Alastair Men

surfing mennie wAVeS

Dad, you are my inspiration.
'If our love could have saved you,
you would have lived forever'

Published by Alastair Mennie

© 2010 Alastair Mennie

Designed by April Sky Design, Newtownards
www.aprilsky.co.uk

Printed by GPS Colour Graphics Limited

ISBN 978-0-9565039-0-9

About the author

Alastair Mennie is a surfer from Northern Ireland specifically involved in big wave surfing. He is inspired by the big wave surfers of California, Hawaii and South Africa. He has been involved in the search for, the discovery of and the pioneering of many big wave surf spots in Ireland. Alastair rode the record breaking swell of December 1st 2007 at Mullaghmore Head, Co. Sligo and has been involved in numerous ground breaking big wave sessions in Ireland. He has competed at International invite only big wave contests and has played a part in illustrating that big waves and the surfers capable of riding them exist further afield than the more traditional shores of the Pacific.

Front Cover – Photo: Aaron Pierce

contents

the mennie brothers

SO THERE I WAS aged 13, sitting in my bedroom that I shared with my younger brother Andrew, in our family's beach side apartment in Castlerock, Northern Ireland. It wasn't plastered in too many surf posters because Mum and Dad didn't want the wallpaper ruined with sticky tape. Instead our walls were covered in very embarrassing 'snatch' the dog blue wallpaper and we had lamp shades, duvets and pillow cases to match! So there we are, Andrew is tucked up in bed, under snatch the dog, and I'm perched on the end of my bed glued to the surf film we had just rented from the local surf shop. 'Monster Mavericks' is a film about the big wave surf spot in Northern California on the northern tip of Half Moon Bay. The spot was pioneered by Jeff Clark alone for 15 years before he could get anyone else to surf with him out there. It was and still is renowned as one of the most deadly and frightening big wave surf locations on the planet, famously claiming the life of Legendary, Hawaiian big wave surfer, Mark Foo. The waves break on a reef submerged under the water a mile off the harbour and in front of jagged rocks. Now maybe you can begin to understand why only one man wanted to surf there for so long.

We were used to watching ordinary surf films of sunshine, blue water and high speed turns. This was something different. The waves were huge, the colours dark and menacing and the surfers clad in lots of rubber. It wasn't until many years later that I realised those were not the only similarities between Northern California and Northern Ireland.

At the age of 13, my brother and I had been surfing for a couple of years already. We started out on boogie boards aged 7 and 9. I think it was my 11th birthday that Mum and dad bought me my first 'pop out' surfboard. It was 7'6" and covered in lots of surf stickers. A 'pop out' surf board is basically a plastic surfboard out of a mould. There is a really funny shot of me standing in the front garden with my arm around the board, wearing a terrible wetsuit and wrap around sunglasses. I must have thought I looked so cool! Although surfing had been in Ireland since the 60's when, to the best of my knowledge, local men; Davey Govan, Alan Duke and Ian Hill first took to the water, it was still very unusual to see another surfer. My family knew so little about surfing that we thought waxing the bottom of the board was the way to go, like snow skis! We had totally no idea that wax was for grip and not for speed!

I couldn't get my arm around my board so Dad had to carry it for me to the edge of the water as Mum and Andrew ran behind me with a lifejacket. Mum made me wear a red life jacket with this big stupid collar on it. If a kid did that nowadays at the beach, he would be laughed off it! Despite looking cool in my wrap around sunglasses and wetsuit that was as comfortable as a cardboard box, the lifejacket didn't bother me and all I was interested in was getting into the surf.

The waves were wind swept and brown. Castlerock beach is right next to the River Bann Estuary. The river has a peat bottom and it stains the water like an auburn colour. It was freezing as it was November, and I remember my wee water skiing gloves that I had from when I was 6, weren't keeping me very warm. I didn't manage to get to my feet that day but I loved the surfboard as opposed to the boogie board. It wasn't long before my brother had his first surfboard too. He got a 5'10 short board from Santa, a month later, and he stood the very first time! I think that was the first time we experienced sibling rivalry! If you have a younger brother or sister and you both take part in the same thing, I'm sure you have an idea of what it must have made me feel when the wee git stood up first time and I didn't! That was the start of it! I would say stuff about his board to make him feel his wasn't as good as mine or he would pretend to not see me do something on a wave when he blatantly did! It's not like that nowadays because we are older but when we were young and into our earlier 20's we were pretty competitive and that probably helped push our surfing through the years.

It's funny looking back on us being that young and just starting out. The way we just learned as we went along. We came up with some pretty weird ways of trying to keep warm in the sea. Andrew was a twig and I wasn't much bigger so we felt the cold when we were little. We both can admit to wearing yellow washing up gloves in the surf and both of us wore two wetsuits from time to time. I will admit to wearing white socks under my booties and Vaseline on my face and hands for a while but Andrew decided when he was 7 that he would wear Coleraine Rugby Club, knee high socks right through until he was 14! He swore by them, it was so funny watching him put these big blue and white stripy socks on in the living room, pull them up to his knees as he stood completely naked before pulling his wetsuit on.

When we were watching 'Monster Mavericks', I said "I want to be able to surf one of those waves some day, one of those big 30footers". I was in awe at the surfers catching gigantic waves on huge surfboards; I was in shock at the wipe-outs and hold downs. All of a sudden all the other videos we had watched seemed erased from my memory. I don't remember Andrew responding to my statement, either because he ignored me or I was so focused on the television that I didn't register it.

We began to hear about contests being run around the entire island of Ireland, north and south by the ISA (Irish Surfing Association) Aged 14 and Andrew 12, we began to do some of them. I remember the first one we did was at Rossnowlagh, in Donegal. It was a full family trip for the weekend. Mum, Dad, Scott the Golden Labrador, that ate way too much, and Andrew and I. Rossnowlagh is a really gentle beach break, perfect for beginners and kids. I entered the under 16 category and Andrew was young enough to enter the under 12 category. I'm sure you can guess what I'm about to say now. That's right, I made it to the quarter finals and where did Andrew come in his category? He won it! First competition and he cleans up! The funny thing about this is that just a week before the contest he had put his board into Troggs Surf Shop with a for sale tag on it as he had decided to give up surfing and keep up boogie boarding instead! I kid you not! He was going to give up surfing then a week later he wins the Irish title in his first event. He also entered the under 18 boogie board that day aged 12 and came 4th! There I am with a quarter final result, which was probably not too bad for my first competition, and that wee git not only wins his Under 12 division but also comes 4th in another! I don't think at the time I realised how competitive and determined I was becoming as a result of this but looking back I can see that those early experiences have shaped a large part of me. He went on to win his age category every year until he was 18 not to mention numerous other events and finals placings. I always did ok, I won a couple of events here and there and placed in the finals most of the time but he was winning things all the time!

Growing up together as surfers was weird for us as we lived outside Hillsborough and went to school in Lisburn which for anyone who doesn't know is about an hour from the north coast. We only had weekends to surf as we always spent weekends and holidays in Mum and Dad's holiday apartment in Castlerock. I think this 'time limit' we had to surf made us appreciate it more than some of our friends who lived in Castlerock full time. I would be up at 6am phoning my friends Andrew Wilson and Ross Olphart trying to get them to come and surf with me but it was usually 8am or so before they came to the beach. Andrew and I however were in the water most of the day and if we weren't in it, we were watching it before going in again.

The one difference between Andrew and I was that I loved going out in bigger waves. He absolutely loved and still does to this day, surfing small waves. He loves it and has never had any interest in surfing bigger waves. I used to paddle out the back at Castlerock and sit for ages waiting on a big set to come through just to get one yet Andrew would be more than content sitting on the 'inside' closer to the beach, were the waves reformed and he'd catch 10 times as many as me and get the same buzz that I would from catching one bigger one.

I would have gone out at the more dangerous reef breaks on my own and surfed when the waves were big. I loved it. I always wanted to be out in the water on the biggest days. I remember surfing a spot which was, at that time, a well kept secret near Bundoran, when I was 16. It was big and nasty. The waves were in the 15foot range on the face. (In surfing there are lots of weird and wonderful ways to measure waves, I use the most obvious, the face height.) I was on my own and I'd had a few waves under my belt when all of a sudden I miss timed catching one. I ended up getting stuck in the lip (the crest of the breaking wave) and pitched out into mid air. I hit my head on my board, thankfully I was wearing a helmet, I then hit the reef with my head and to finish me off, the wave smashed me into the reef. If you can imagine a diver going off a high board like a sack of spuds, then that is pretty much what I must have looked like. I didn't have time to think about throwing in a summersault with a tuck to add to my performance. I ended up in Hospital the next day with whiplash! Yes whiplash, my neck was solid and they made me do exercises with a bin liner on my pillow. I felt pretty stupid but a little macho at the same time!

At the age of 18 and Andrew 16, we moved into this old house that my Dad had bought as a building site in Castlerock. My Dad was a builder. Many of the men on his side of the family were trawler men and in fact he used to work on the boats when he was younger. Dad was from Glasgow and he moved over to Northern Ireland with his Mum after his Father died suddenly aged 60. Dad was only 16 when he lost his Dad and he and his Mum came to Northern Ireland shortly after his death. Dad worked on the trawlers and eventually got into the building trade which turned out to be his passion. He had bought a site in Castlerock and planned to build a house on it for him and Mum to retire to. In the meantime though there was an old house on the site. An elderly woman had passed away before dad bought it so it was really old worldly inside and had that musty elderly person scent about it. Andrew and I didn't care about that or the fact that there were no carpets anywhere, the main thing we were concerned about was the fact that you could see the sea from every room and the beach was literally about 50feet away from the front wall! We moved in with Scott the dog, thankfully the snatch the dog bedding had long gone at this stage! I set up a gym in the spare room as I was really into my cross training for surfing and we each had a bedroom overlooking the sea. We were pretty lucky having that to live in at such a young age! We both were studying construction at the local technical college and I had a job working as a computer aided design technician in an Engineering practice in nearby Coleraine.

Having a job and studying meant I had to be really efficient with my time if I was to keep on improving at my surfing. I used to go to tech on a Monday all day until 8pm with a lunch and dinner break then work four days a week until 5:30pm. I became super efficient with managing my time and I was able to surf in the mornings, go to work, surf for 20mins in my lunch break and then after work too. That's three surfs a day and still working a 9-5! In the winter it was more difficult to get the third surf in as it was dark at 4pm but there were times I would have gone in at West Strand as the lights on the promenade would give me just enough light to see the waves. Not the smartest thing to do but that's what I did!

We were starting to get a name for ourselves and soon became known as 'The Surfers' to locals around the town. We were getting articles in the local papers and television coverage. 'The Mennie Brothers' as we became known were standing out as people who surfed and also as muckers! A friend of mine once said that a great program could be made if someone was to follow us around with a video camera. We were a couple of pranksters, always having a laugh and messing around. There wasn't much that people would put past us. We were always up to something.

BOTH ANDREW AND I knew that in order to progress at our surfing we needed more exposure to better surfers. We lived in Castlerock on the North Coast and there were only a couple of other surfers who we rarely ever saw and they were quite a bit older than us. We wanted to take our surfing further and we had been doing the Irish contests for some time at this stage and felt it was time to step it up a little.

We both had sponsors since we were really young but that was not going to be enough to help us improve our surfing. In fact I was sponsored by a company called 'Circle One' who where based in Exeter, England, and Andrew was sponsored by 'Bodyglove' who were based in Plymouth. We both also had a deal from Devon surfboard shapers 'Gulfstream'. Mum and Dad always took care of us and we were lucky to have their support at all times and I am really grateful for that. We wanted to try and push ourselves against other good surfers. We had been on loads of family holidays to France and Portugal etc and we knew that we were probably as capable as the average French or Portuguese guy so this gave us a bit of scope on what was possible.

We both enrolled on a construction management degree course at The University of Plymouth, England. The reason of course was that Plymouth was by the sea, in Devon, right next to Cornwall. We knew that if we wanted to absorb ourselves in surfing then we had to be there and the smartest way to do this was to do a degree at the same time! Plymouth University Surf Club was renowned for its good surf team. They always had a couple of top UK surfers on their team and the team, more often than not, won The British University Title.

Andrew and I had a wee car between us and we used to go to the beach at Newquay and other local beaches. For those of you who don't know, Newquay is the heart of British Surfing. It is the Huntington Beach of the British Isles. It is where a lot of surf brands are based and a lot of surfers in the UK mags are pretty much based there too. It also was where the BPSA (British Professional Surfing Association Tour) was based which is one of the main reasons I personally went to England.

Surfers around the area started to notice us. It was difficult not to, we are both 6'5" tall with red hair and the Northern Irish accent stood out. In fact it stood out so much people couldn't understand me when I would go into a shop. The amount of times people asked me to repeat myself was ridiculous; I began to wonder if I was speaking a different language! I even began speaking in an English accent when I was ordering food or I would get a friend to speak for me! I lived in a pretty rough area of the city. There was a wee corner shop among all the terraced houses, on route from uni, which I would go into to get a Cornish pasty from time to time. A Cornish pasty is a traditional food in Cornwall. It is basically a pastry folded in half and filled with meat and vegetables and sometimes can have half of it savoury and half of it sweet. It has a big crust on it so the tin miners could eat it without getting it dirty down the mine. (There's your history lesson for the day). It was great after a surf. The girl in the shop thought I was German! I thought she would have got used to me coming in and getting a pasty and learned to not bother listening to what I was asking for and just get me one out but she didn't and therefore every time I went in I would put on my best English accent and it worked a treat!

I was never much of a partier; anyone who knows me will tell you that. I was never really into drinking and I never smoked or took drugs despite all my friends being into drinking. My brother on the other hand was the complete opposite to me in this respect. He could drink for both of us! Most people associate students with drinking and to be honest that is a huge part of going to university for a lot of people. My brother fitted right into that scene and loved the parties etc. I was different. I was happier sitting in my room just chilling as I would want to be getting up early to drive to the surf and back before class started. I lived in a building owned by the university. I had my own little room with a bathroom that was like one you would see on an airplane and a kitchen you couldn't swing a cat in! I was on the top floor and if I fully opened my window and hung out to my waist I could just see the sea across the buildings. There was a water sports store downstairs where I kept my boards and wetsuits. I had a range of 'short boards' and I had a 7'4" for bigger waves. (A short board is what we would call a board that was built for high performance surfing as opposed to a 'long board' which is more of a traditional type of surfing. Short boards can be any length really but they are shaped to be surfed technically and at speed. Boards over 7'6" are for bigger waves and then long boards are generally over 9'2" and have a rounded nose. I could go into way more detail but you would probably fall asleep). I would have ridden my 7'4" board at home in bigger waves and I brought it with me to Plymouth in the hope that I could use it there.

On the same floor of the building I hung out with two Americans, Ryan Glass and Ernie Capbert. Those two guys were so funny and they taught me so much. They were both a little older than me and were both larger than life. Ryan was a big guy, very friendly and really good fun. Ernie was half Puerto Rican, liked to work out and was really into sport. Ernie definitely saw that I wanted to do well in surfing and he helped me psychologically as he had played American football and understood sport I suppose. It was like I had all of a sudden met someone who could relate to me.

I went to Plymouth on a mission. I wasn't there to study although that was the only reason I was able to be there. I went there to improve my surfing and compete against all the guys I would normally see in magazines or from time to time at European or World events. I wanted to make a mark. It wasn't like I wanted to see how good I could get; it was more like I was going there to confirm that I was as good as other surfers.

Andrew went to Plymouth with exactly the same goal in mind. We were going to surf and make a mark. I had blinkers on to anything else going on at uni. I always did my work and I didn't neglect my studies but I mean I was blinkered to anything other than that. I wasn't interested in going to the pub; I wasn't interested in being in clubs or societies or going on pub crawls. I had such focus that nothing was capable of interfering with my mind set. My brother wasn't like that. Andrew loved partying and socialising etc and really loved the student lifestyle. He was the life and soul of the party and people loved his antics. He didn't neglect his surfing or his studies either but he didn't really surf as much as I thought he was going to. Some people might say that I missed out on a lot of experiences by being so blinkered with my surfing but I think I have gained more unique experiences through following my heart than if I had tried to be something I was not.

Andrew and I are similar in a lot of ways and up until this point in our lives we pretty much did everything together. When we went to university, things started to change and different aspects of each of our personalities began to strengthen or weaken.

The moment I noticed the difference in Andrew and I still stands out in my mind today. It was 630am on a Saturday morning, late October. I was standing outside his window, beneath a street light. Andrew and I lived in different buildings about a mile apart. The street ran slightly uphill between two purpose built blocks of student accommodation. It was dead, no one around, just me standing in the centre of the road in the dark. I was calling his mobile phone and throwing stones at his window. The entire street was silent, obviously it had been a big night and everyone was still in bed. We had arranged to leave at 6.30am for a contest in Croyde, Devon. I called about 100 times and waited for 15 minutes but he never showed up. We had to leave at 630am as we had a 90 minute drive to Croyde ahead of us and check in was at 830am. This turned out to be the first of many times that I ended up going to contests on my own!

I started doing some of the contests and I was doing ok. Though, when I started on The BPSA Tour I couldn't get it together. I remember going to one in Langland Bay, Wales and just freezing up as everyone in the heat was ripping it up all around me. I kind of felt a bit overwhelmed as I hadn't really been around a lot of good surfers all the time. I was used to not seeing many decent surfers at home. I started to over think the whole thing and before I knew it I was just sitting there getting beaten without even putting up a fight.

I remember standing in the car park that night crying down the phone to Mum and Dad. I was so frustrated with myself. I just couldn't seem to get it together and was getting beaten fair and square but I felt I was only surfing to about 20% of my ability. This was a turning point for me and from this moment on I began to get really serious about it. I knew that for me to be happy and content I needed to surf my best and give myself the best chance or I would be miserable. I didn't want to get beaten without surfing to the best of my ability, I didn't want to feel like I was no good when I knew I was capable of at least making the finals at the events if not the final four. So far all that happened was I was getting knocked out in the early rounds.

I drove back to Plymouth that night in howling winds and rain thinking about what I was going to do. That was the last contest of the season so I had a bit of time to get myself sorted out.

The contest season always opened at the beginning of March at Fistral beach, Newquay with The British University Championships. Believe it or not, this is one of the biggest surf contest in the world with over 700 entries every year from all over the British Isles. Every University could enter a team made up of both men and women. I set my sights on this event and the BPSA Tour. I planned to have sorted myself out by then. I again started to use my time efficiently so that I could go my classes, study, surf, and training in the gym and most importantly sort my head out. I began to realise that it wasn't so much my surfing ability that was holding me back and more so my head and self belief. I started going to the gym at 6.30am every day and as well as surfing I worked on my mind. I went to the library and looked through some sports psychology books. I even bought a subliminal sports tape that I put on while I studied. I developed my own way of making myself believe in me through writing key words on paper and sticking them on my walls, in my wallet on the screen saver of my phone and computer. I basically wanted to surround myself in positivity as much as possible. I am sure I didn't do well in that Wales contest because I didn't believe in myself. I didn't believe I was as good as them and therefore just gave up.

The next few months I did all this training and both my brother and I were picked for the university A team to compete at the nationals. Andrew was always a very natural surfer and it was effortless for him. I always had to work hard and he would just turn up and still do well. Dad always said "If there was a brick wall, I would break the wall down and get through it, whereas Andrew would open the door and meet me on the other side!" Before I moved to Plymouth I knew that if you made that team then you were obviously doing quite well. However I just saw being picked for the team as part of the course of winning the event. I had my sights set on winning; I didn't for a second ever consider any other place as being an option. I knew who my competition was and I was on a mission. Being 6'5 I used to struggle to get the right boards for me to surf really small waves. Both Andrew and I have always been quite unusual in our size and therefore getting boards made took slightly longer to get the right shape to suit our surfing. Being in England, made me have to learn to surf in really sloppy conditions to do well in contests as generally contest conditions were poor. I had to get the right equipment and learn how to use it properly. The waves in England tended to be a little more gutless than what I was used to at home so I had to widen and fatten up my boards to stop me bogging down in small surf.

When March came round I had completed all my training, I had been through every scenario a million times, I had the right boards and I knew I was capable of dealing with whatever came my way. I learned from past experiences with the Irish team that staying with a team was not good for me so I booked myself into a hotel on my own. In fact the contest fell on the same day that an Irish Team Selection event took place. There was no way in hell I was giving up this opportunity to go and take part in an Irish team event. I had already represented Ireland numerous times at various World and European competitions. The Newquay event meant so much more to me.

There are so many people in this event that there are 7 rounds before the finals! The competition level may not be very high at all except for a handful of good surfers but 7 rounds was a lot of chances to get knocked out for a silly mistake! Sure enough, I won my first round heat but in the second round I nearly lost it all! The waves were really sloppy and I struggled to get a decent wave until the last couple of seconds and I scraped through to the next round in second. I went on to win all the other heats and then I took the individual title and helped Plymouth A team secure overall first place. I was so stoked! I went straight to the pay phone and told Mum and Dad and I will never forget them screaming down the phone! I will never forget Dad telling me "you can do it son!" the night before the contest and to be able to phone them and tell them I had just won was an amazing feeling. Andrew didn't do as well as he had hoped and went out in round four. Conditions were difficult. Surfing isn't like football where you put on a pair of boots, get a ball and take it to a level playing field. Every wave is different, you need a selection of boards to chose from to suit any given conditions and its not easy to practice one move again and again as the waves change every second even when you have caught one. It's not always the best surfer that wins a contest for this reason!

I had won! I was so happy, all my hard work had paid off and I felt great! All the local media were interviewing me and when I went home the Northern Irish media were too. To the best of my knowledge I was the first Northern Irish surfer to ever win a British title. I was stoked and it did heaps for my confidence.

I went on that year to win another Student title at Watergate Bay and I finished 5th over all on The BPSA Tour. I learned a lot from these experiences about me, who I am, what it takes for me to achieve things and what I'm capable of.

I was at university in Plymouth, doing the contests and generally surfing as much as I possibly could for two years. I also travelled to

France, Spain and Portugal a fair bit to do some of the WQS Tour events. The WQS Tour (World Qualifying Series Tour) is the next stage up from the BPSA. The WQS is a world tour of contests in which the top 16 overall competitors make it onto the WCT (World Championship Tour). Now if you're not a surfer you probably have just got completely lost with all the abbreviations there. It reminds me a bit of Northern Irish Politics, there's always another party or group with their name abbreviated to a three letter word and it's impossible to keep up with what exactly each party represents. Anyway, very basically, The BPSA is a British version of the world tour. The top world tour surfers' surf on the championship tour and they qualified to be there through the WQS tour.

Andrew and I went and did a few of the events every year since I was about 17. It was such a mission. The events were so far apart and we would be driving through northern Spain to get to Tapia in Galicia at night as the roads were so bad it made more sense to drive when everyone was in bed. We didn't ever do too well in these events, the standard of surfers was much higher and their judging system demanded more from us than we had ever experienced. It turned out that these contests turned into experiences to remember for other reasons rather than the events themselves standing out to us if you know what I mean. For example, we got on a train one year from Biarritz to Hossegor to do a contest at Capreton. We used to travel with a big coffin board bag each (this is a big padded bag holding more than one board.) I think we had about three boards each with us so that we had back ups should we break one or conditions were changeable. These bags are pretty heavy, so we strapped a skateboard to the bottom of each with duct tape and luggage straps and pulled them around with us. I remember getting on an empty bus in Santander one time with the bags and putting them across the seats at the back window, out of the way. Before we knew it the bus was packed with elderly Basque Ladies. All the seats were filled and Andrew and I were standing in the aisle among about 20 sweating old women, who were obviously cursing us and our 8foot friends. Sorry, Got side tracked there. We got to the contest site at Capreton and we set up our tent, near to the judging podium, on the top of the sand dune alongside a Basque family that always went to the same events as us. That night I wakened up at 1am to Andrew going nuts, Spanish singing, a girl crying, howling winds, torrential rain and lightening. If you have ever seen one of these electrical storms in France then you will know how scary they are. I got out of the tent to try and hold it down while Andrew sat inside using his weight to keep it on the ground. There I am, lying face down on top of this sand dune in my green and white spotted boxer shorts with my arms spread eagle holding onto the corners of the tent. Next to me I could see the whole Basque crew silhouetted in the lightening singing at the top of their voices to comfort the only girl with them. The rain was lashing down from big black clouds, my boxers were clinging to me, soaking wet. I lay there for about 30mins or so until the storm seemed to weaken.

The next day was a scorcher. I remember it distinctly being abnormally hot. The surf was small but the surface was really glassy and still. That night the contest directors allowed us and the Basque crew to stay in one of the marquee tepee tents in case the weather got bad again. These tents were made from a steel frame with a wooden floor laid on top of it. They had steel uprights in the corner and into the roof and a tarpaulin wrapped around the frame and tied together with rope thread through eyelets. The judging podium was basically a portacabin with glazing on the seaward side. It was situated right next to the edge of the sand dune for the best view of the contest area, just above our tent. Behind it was a steep path down to the car park. I remember being beside the podium and looking across the sea towards Spain, normally Spain and the mountains were easily visible from Capreton. However I noticed how Spain had gone and there was just blackness in its place.

It was pretty clear the scorching day was about to turn wet so Andrew and I decided to go and use the pay phone at the end of the car park to ring home before the rain hit. On our way back and half way up the sand dune, an English competitor, came running past shouting "Run!" Andrew and I just sort of smiled and laughed at him as he legged it past us down the hill. Soon we realised everyone was coming down the hill.

We started to run but continued up the hill. When we got over the top and saw the sea and the horizon it was obvious why they were running. The sea was all choppy now and the waves all broken up. The wind was blowing off the sea and pretty much everyone had left the beach. We started to run down the path to the beach against the strengthening wind towards the tent. The path was basically cut into the front of the sand dune. Andrew was slightly ahead of me. All of a sudden the wind hit full on and we were knocked onto the ground. We both ended up on the sand with sand being whipped up everywhere and rain was starting to fall too. The rain was sore, it wasn't like a wee drizzle it was like big drops of water hitting us. We got up and made it to the tepee tent, the opening of which was facing towards the storm.

The Basque crew were trying to weave the eyelets together with rope to keep it shut. We slipped into the opening at the bottom between their father's legs. He was wearing a pair of shorts, no top and standing with his back to the storm holding an edge of the tarpaulin in each hand while the rest of the family tried to weave the rope between the eyelets. The old man was screaming in agony as the rain turned to hail and the winds got stronger and started pelting the hail at his back. Andrew and I tried to take the tarpaulin and hold it for him. All of a sudden the wind broke in through a corner in the tent ripping one of the uprights out of its base. There were five of the Basque crew and two of us all spread along the side of the tent trying to hold it down. One of the kids was about 16, wearing only white Y fronts and laughing in hysterics as all our boards and the tables got pinned against the far side wall of the tent by the wind. I think we all knew what was about to happen but we weren't giving in. Sure enough the opposite upright then snapped from the base. The wooden slab at the bottom was pulled up to about 45 degrees and everyone started sliding off the edge into the sand. I don't know what I was thinking but I jumped up and clung onto a cross bar and tried to hold it down! I must have thought I was superman for a second. I could hear Andrew shouting "let go Al, let go!" I did and slid down the wooden base and off to the side. The whole tent, frame and everything took off up the coast. It was like a sandstorm, we couldn't see anything. We edged our way back up the sand dune until all of a sudden, like a switch going off, the storm passed. I remember getting to the podium and opening the door and everyone inside burst out laughing as we were caked in sand. They couldn't believe that the tent they saw take off down the beach had us in it! Then round the corner comes 'Y front boy'. He wasn't laughing now, he was shouting for his family. (Broken English accent) "Where are my family, my family, where are my family?" He was plastered in sand; his white y fronts looked more like he'd done a number two in them as they were now brown! All our stuff, passports, boards, everything was gone. We could see parts of the tent scattered the whole way up the beach so we started walking along gathering bits and pieces as we went. We eventually got most of our stuff back. We got a newspaper the next day and realised that the front page photograph of a lamp post through the roof of a car was caused by the storm. The paper was reporting a tornado had passed through from the coast and into Bayonne causing havoc and devastation. We got lucky with just a few things lost in the sand!

CHAPTER 3

tragedy

IT WAS JULY 3rd 2003 and I was at a birthday dinner party in a restaurant in Plymouth. I had just flown in from Belfast earlier that day as I had been at home for about a week since finishing my 2nd year exams. I remember putting my phone onto silent. I remember specifically doing it as it was something I never used to do. I always had the volume on in case someone needed to contact me. You never know when you may be someone's only point of contact and they might need your help! I was sitting at a table of about 12 people and I think we were about to have desert when I checked my phone. I had no less than ten missed calls. I immediately wondered who on earth could be ringing me that many times?! I pressed the button on the screen to bring up the caller id and it turned out to be our landline number at home in Northern Ireland. I thought this seemed a bit strange so I phoned back right away without even leaving the table. I was expecting Mum or Dad to answer but when another man answered I started to wonder who it could have been. The gruff country voice said "Alastair, is that you?" I replied "Yeah". I was still confused as to who it was. I could hear others in the back ground. The voice continued "I'll put you onto your Mum". I waited for Mum to come on the line and the first thing she said was "Alastair, your Dad's dead son" I paused very briefly and got up from my seat and began to walk towards the door of the restaurant. "Ok" I said, "Who is with you, does Andrew Know?" I went into overdrive. I didn't stop for a second to take stock of what was going on, I just stepped straight into being strong for Mum.

I got on the next flight home that night from Bristol airport. I cried in the airport but I made a conscious decision that I was going to be the rock for the family. I was going to take over where Dad left off, no matter what that took. We were all devastated. Dad died at only 50 years of age very suddenly at home. We were completely unprepared for it; well I suppose you can't ever prepare for something like that. My theory was if I broke down then Mum and Andrew will too. They need to see strength and Dad was always our strength, our rock. If he was gone then I knew that I had to step up and take control of everything and maintain stability in the family. I was 22 at the time. I was just another surf bum student and all of a sudden I had to grow up, quickly. I now had Mum and Andrew to think of, the family business and so much else to do, let alone grieve myself. I went about dealing with it all in a selfless way I suppose although I didn't realise that at the time. My main priority was Mum and Andrew. I needed to make sure they saw strength and then they would be strong. Then, the business, I needed to make sure that was under control. I was somehow able to not think about myself or my feelings too much and keep control of the situation.

I remember going into the funeral hall. All three of us walked across the front of the room and into a side room where Dad was. I stepped in front of Mum and Andrew so as they would see it was ok to go in. I hadn't considered what it might be like to see my Dad and I nearly collapsed. I remember nearly passing out but somehow I refused to do that. I couldn't weaken at this point. I kept my head up and held up Mum and Andrew. It was intense and I was fighting back my emotions the entire time but I know if I had have let that slip, Mum and Andrew may have broken down even more. I don't know how I did it, but I even wrote a poem for Dad and some how managed to read it without breaking down. I suppose I was in overdrive and that made me block everything out. All of a sudden my surfing seemed to be a miniscule part of my life as it was smothered with the tragedy of losing my father.

The next few weeks were filled with emptiness and chaos, if that makes sense? The emptiness of not having Dad there to ask what to do and the chaos of trying to ground everything that was thrown into the air. I have never seen anyone in as much pain as I saw my Mum in at that time. It was shocking. I will never forget it. It was like she was ripped in two. I don't know how she didn't have a heart attack to be honest; it must be horrific when all of a sudden your husband passes away and your life is shattered. Even as I write this it is obvious to me that I'm still thinking of them before myself, maybe that's a sign that I still haven't had time to deal with it all myself, I don't know, time will tell.

From this moment forward, all our lives changed dramatically. Though I can only speak in detail of my own life and feelings, it was obvious how everyone else was affected. I took on the 'man of the family' role. I remember one day a business colleague of Dads' phoned the house to ask how we were getting on. He said "You are really grasping the nettle Alastair!" I'd never heard this expression before but at the time I took it as meaning taking the bull by the horns. Not only was I trying to keep Mum and Andrew together but the business too. Dad owned a building company which was in the middle of a development at the time. I knew the foreman, Francie as he had been with Dad for a long time. Francie came to the house as soon as he heard the news, in fact he was there before I was. I remember standing in the living room with Francie talking to various people about the business. The living room had an amazing view, through huge windows, across the hills to Belfast. It had a solid marble floor and on the ceiling was a compass made from timber.

I used to love this room and I remember always thinking about where north was on the compass and working out where the wind was blowing from. Francie and I stood in there and I was listening to everyone talking about what was going to happen with the business and how we were going to go about closing it up and selling it off. It was almost like I wasn't there. Andrew was in the other room with Mum at the time and as everyone stood in the living room discussing what will happen it was like they had forgotten I was standing there and that maybe I had something to say. Francie was standing on my right and an agent was talking to us. Francie is a country man. You know what I mean, hands like shovels, built like an ox. The agent was smartly dressed in a grey suit and over weight. The agent said he will find a buyer and for us not to worry. I'm sure he was only trying to help and reassure us that it will be taken care of and to take it off our minds. It was a bit annoying to be honest, Dad was only gone a matter of hours and it felt like vultures were already circling. I wasn't prepared to just let it go that easy. I said, "I will be taking the business on". The agent didn't really say much; in fact I don't remember him saying anything at all after I made that statement. Francie was behind me all the way. He said, "You can do this Alastair, your Dad didn't build this up and put you two through education for it all to be sold off!" I agreed.

Francie was the only one that openly was in support of me. No one else said a word but I could see it in their faces and in their actions that they didn't like it for some reason. Maybe they were just scared for me as they knew I probably wasn't aware of what I was getting into. I spoke to Mum about it and she agreed to let me take it on and at least sort it out for her. I wasn't going to let this slip from us and I wasn't about to let the vultures take it from us either. I knew none of us were in any state of mind to be making any decisions about, well, anything so I figured it was best to keep a hold of things until the situation smoothed out a little and we could see more clearly.

I studied construction at university for a total of four years though I had only ever been on site a couple of times for field trips. I was only ever on site with Dad three times that I can remember. Once as a child, once cleaning out houses before handover and once to mark out the foundations for a new house. That was it. In 22 years, with a Dad as a builder, I had only been on site three times! That may sound ridiculous but when I thought about it, my friends Dad is a mechanic yet he didn't know how to change a wheel on his car and I had to do it for him! Studying construction definitely helped as I knew what was going on but I severely lacked experience though I was sure I was about to gain that pretty quickly.

I remember three days after the funeral, Andrew and I went to the site. Two of the plasterers were actually there. Dad had a workforce of men, most of who had been with him for many years and knew Mum well too. The plasterers were two brothers from Co. Down. Malachy and Eugene were their names. I went up to them and they said "We just had to come in and finish it off for him." They were doing the last patching on a newly built house. I remember almost crying. I was touched at how dedicated they were to Dad. Andrew and I began to mark out the next house on the site. This would have taken Dad about five minutes but it took us about 3hours. We deliberately went there when there was no one around. The site was dead, lifeless, just a digger sitting there like the driver had just abandoned it and any of the houses that were lived in seemed to be empty at the time. We spent three hours with a bag of lime, a bunch of steel pins and a drawing, trying to mark out the walls on the ground so the digger driver could dig the foundations. I felt completely in the dark, alone and isolated. Andrew was with me but I really felt like we were abandoned and completely lost as where to even start, though we carried on and eventually got it marked out, all of which was correct from memory except one wall which Francie noticed and fixed for us.

I remember the first surf Andrew and I had after Dad died. We went to Portballintrae on a Sunday afternoon, a week after the funeral. I felt really bad for leaving Mum but she had others around her. It wasn't like I was going surfing for fun; it was a release from reality. It was somewhere for me to be and leave everything on the beach before I paddled out. I was full of anger at this stage. I was angry at what had happened to Dad. The car park at Portballintrae over looks the bay and in the distance a huge stately home converted into apartments, right next to The Giants Causeway. The car park was pretty busy that day as it is a favourite with second home owners from Belfast and as it was July, all the kids were off school at the beach. I remember meeting Barry (Baz) Johnston there. I knew Baz from surfing but he wasn't a really close friend at that time. He had heard from others who were at the funeral that Dad had gone and he offered his condolences to us both. A few other surfers we knew did the same. When I went into the water, the surf was pumping, head high and clean. Everyone was having a good surf but it was pretty packed with beginners and tourists. I felt like I couldn't surf properly because I couldn't concentrate and I felt like everyone was looking at me. I didn't want to make eye contact with anyone. I wished I had gone somewhere else to surf on my own and before long I was back on the beach heading for the car park. I just couldn't get into it. My head was too full of other things and although I needed a surf to try and wash away some of what I had been feeling, I actually ended up feeling worse.

My life routine began to change. Instead of coming home from uni for the summer before going into my final year, I was instead trying to grasp a business of which I knew very little about. I began to make plans to continue my studies part time but that didn't work out. I had one more year to do. I even began flying over for lectures and flying back. I then tried to finish the course at home alongside learning the business. I knew how much it meant to have a degree and I also knew dad always said, as long as I could get my degree finished then I could do whatever I wanted as I had that as back up forever. I slowly began to realise that it wasn't going to be possible to keep it going and I had to focus on the business and get to grips with it. This was a weird realisation for me as all of a sudden I had to start making huge decisions without having my father there to bounce ideas off.

I slowly developed a routine where I was on site most of the time but if the waves were good I would go and surf. It was weird sitting in Dads' chair in his office, using his notes and his pens to run his business without him looking over my shoulder helping me. I had to kind of put the pieces of the jigsaw together and work out what was going on and then make decisions. I spoke to his business associates and Mum a lot trying to get my head around the whole thing. Eventually I managed to work out my place in the running of the whole business and develop a way to fit in my own time into my new life too. It was definitely a shock to the system but somehow I adapted to my new role.

I was fitting work around surfing and surfing around work as well looking after Mum. Andrew decided he should go back to uni and finish his degree. He didn't want to get into the business at that time and we thought that if he was to go and finish it then when he had graduated he could come back and at least he would have a business to go into right away. So between Mum and I we managed to keep it all going. I took on a lot more of it than Mum to be honest, I wanted to let her have time to grieve in peace so I just got on with it.

My surfing began to take a different direction too. I was enjoying being back at home where the waves had power and size. The 7'4" that I took to Plymouth didn't even get wet over there and I was gagging to get into some meaty waves on it. Although I had been loving life in Plymouth and doing the contests I missed the bigger surf we have at home. There were only really a couple of days when I was there that got my heart racing if you know what I mean. I was longing for a solid swell. I used to paddle for ages through lines of white water at Castlerock to get out beyond the waves. Sometimes it was so big it would be breaking way out beyond the end of the pier. Castlerock has a big stone jetty at the eastern end of it which is used as a retaining wall to keep the channel at the mouth of the River Bann open for boats to get through. I couldn't say exactly how long it is but it juts out into the sea a good 400yrds or so. I used to sit out the back and catch the biggest waves I could. Mum and Dad would have watched me from the window of the apartment through a telescope. Dad loved always having a telescope in the house. Occasionally Dad would walk up the beach and watch me from the pier. If you stand on the pier when the surf is big, the waves smash up over the end and you can get a pretty good view of any surfers in the water as you are raised up above the surf and closer to the surfers.

It felt like I hadn't used my 7'4" in ages. Even to pick it up and feel it in my hands made me hungry for bigger waves. It just felt beefier and longer than what I had been using in England recently. I tried to continue doing the BPSA Tour contests by flying over all the time and I still kept up decent results finishing 7th over all but I was getting frustrated as I knew I could be doing better. I was frustrated as I hadn't been training the way I did previously and it was definitely showing in my confidence and performance. It wasn't long until I made the decision that enough was enough. I decided I would rather bow out than fade out. I was so tired and at one stage I was flying over every weekend for three weeks in a row to a contest somewhere in England or Scotland. It was taking it out of me as I was working all week, still trying to find my feet and then Friday night on a plane, compete all weekend then fly back Sunday night and into work on the Monday again. I was mentally and emotionally drained and my performance had deteriorated.

Meanwhile all this was going on; I was finding my passion for bigger waves. It was coming to the forefront of my mind as being in England had suppressed the love I had for it as I was so focused on doing the contests at the time. My Dad died on July 3rd 2003 and the last conversation I had with him, the day before, was about what I was going to do in the future. It was a really sunny afternoon and we were in the front garden in Annahilt. Dad had built a big pond (it was more like a lake actually, you could have done laps up and down it!), Dad was sitting on a sun lounger on a raised timber deck he had built at the side of it which was surrounded in trees and plants. I was just dandering around the edge of the pond talking to him pretty casually. I said how I wanted to go and surf Mavericks and that maybe if I went to California I might be able to work over there in construction or maybe I could teach surfing or something. Dad was always really supportive. It was very rarely he would ever say no to something unless he thought there was a really good reason why. He did say Mum wouldn't like that idea but if I wanted to do it then I should go but to take it seriously and be careful. We talked on for a bit more about how lots of buildings in the states were built from timber and they still used imperial measurements and that I would have to adjust to that if I wanted to work there. As you can imagine, this conversation spurred me on once Dad had died. I knew I had his blessing to surf what is still regarded as one of the, if not the most deadly places on earth. This meant he thought I had it in me, he thought I was capable. I'm sure this is one of the reasons why Mum tolerates it now and doesn't try and stop me from doing it even though she hates it.

SHORTLY AFTER DADS DEATH, my long time friend Emmet O'Doherty phoned me up to try and get me to go on a surf trip with him. Emmet is a first class guy. He is born and bred in Bundoran. Bundoran is a coastal town in Co. Donegal. It is a typical seaside resort that's bustling in the summer and quiet in the winter. It has a back drop of stunning mountains and greenery which run down into rugged slabs of rock and into the dark blue ocean. Emmet actually went to Plymouth uni at the same time as me to study architecture. He is a little older than me so he was in his final year when I was just starting so we only hung out for that year. I have known him and his family for years, actually since I was about 14 I think as I remember going to Wales on the Irish team with his sister Aine. Emmet is a sensible, well educated guy with a hint of madness glistening behind his glasses. He is about 6 foot tall and stocky in build. He comes from a well respected family in Bundoran and pretty much anyone in the town knows them. Looking back now he was probably being a good mate by trying to get me to do things to take my mind off everything. I said I would think about it. I phoned him back a few days later and told him where we were going. That's right, I phoned him to tell him that we were going to Mavericks, Half Moon Bay, California. He was like "Are you serious sham?" (Sham is a slang word, a bit like dude or man I suppose. I think it comes from Ballyshannon, a town just outside Bundoran, and it seems that everyone who surfs around there loves to use it). I told him I was serious but I think he knew that anyway. We spoke for about half an hour about it and knew that we had to plan it properly and work out the best way of doing it.

I looked into boards. I looked at old photos I had in magazines and I studied the Monster Mavs video I had from when I was 13. I knew I needed something pretty big to catch one of those waves at Mavericks. I eventually came up with a few different designs and I asked Jeff at Circle One to make them for me. He made 6 boards, all were in the range of 8'6" to 9'6". Now, if you don't know surfing then this won't mean much unless you consider the fact that an ordinary short board is usually around 6'0" to 6'4" in length. So these boards were much bigger. They weren't classed as traditional long boards, they were classed as 'Big Wave Guns' or 'Rhino Chasers'. Boards built to hunt down and ride huge waves. We had 6 made of different constructions and lengths so I had a variety of boards to use when I got there and if I broke any then I'd have spares. There were plenty of boards so Emmet didn't need to worry about getting any for himself, we just planned on using those ones. When they arrived they weren't exactly what I had planned. They had fin set ups which I wasn't happy about and their plan shape wasn't too good either but they had the length and the thickness we needed so we figured they would do the job although something in the back of my mind kept telling me they weren't going to big enough. Seriously if any surfer sees a 9'6" gun and then I told them its not big enough they would think there was something wrong with me as that is truly a huge board by anyone's standards but I kept my mind open to the possibility of picking up a second hand one over there from another Mavs surfer.

We knew that Mavericks was in prime time big wave season from about November to February. The biggest waves tended to break in that period every year so we needed to time our trip to be there during that window in the calendar. Both of us worked so it made sense to book it for around Christmas time when the construction sites were closed for two weeks and this coincided perfectly with the Northern Californian winter. We actually booked it for almost four weeks over the Christmas period and into the New Year. Organising this was quite stressful for me as I had to leave Mum with the business for two whole weeks while I was gone and I was a bit worried about it but she was adamant that I had to go as I needed a break from everything. I didn't utter a word of it to any of the workers as I didn't want them thinking they could slack as I wasn't there. I just said nothing. In fact Emmet and I agreed to say nothing to anyone about our planned trip except a couple of close friends each. This was because this was quite an unusual thing to want to do. Most people I knew went on trips to Indonesia or Australia; Mavericks didn't cross people's minds. Looking back on it now, we were definitely taking a huge step for that time in Irish surfing. I knew if word got out that we were planning to surf Mavericks people would laugh at us, slate us and it would spread like wild fire as it was such an unusual thing to want to do. Somehow a few people found out about it and I remember one guy on a boogie board paddling past me in the water at Portballintrae about four weeks before we went saying "Mavericks! eh Mennie?! You're gonna be coming back in a box mate, you're off your head!" That is exactly the reason why I kept my mouth shut about it. I knew no one would even consider it possible that I could do it.

I had been surfing a lot of bigger waves in the coming months before our trip. I had been out to newer spots a little further off the beaten track but what I really needed was a couple of solid swells to shake me up a bit and basically scare me before I went to California. It didn't happen like that though. That's the difficult thing with surfing. In something like football where you might have a big game in say three months, there is a lot of preparation you can do before hand and you know when the match is going to happen. With this, yeah ok we knew when we were going but some proper big wave experience would have been of benefit for sure but at that time there weren't too many places on earth that had been discovered that came close to the ferocity of the ocean at Mavericks, especially in Europe. Big Wave spots were more or less; Mavericks, Jaws and Waimea in Hawaii, Todos Santos Island in Mexico and Dungeons, South Africa. That was it, if you wanted to surf big waves you had to go there. That was just a given as far as I can remember. We spent most of our time training in the gym or swimming. The only thing that came close to proper big waves was a stormy day at East Strand in Portrush where I paddled out and just put myself in the impact zone and took waves on the head. This might sound ridiculous but it was all I had to work with.

Don't get me wrong, I wasn't going to Mavericks with no idea of what I was doing, I'd been in some pretty hairy situations already from surfing sizey waves at home and abroad. I had probably surfed waves as big as 25 ft on the face by the time I was 17 and paid my dues for doing so. I had my wetsuit ripped to my ankles in Tenerife after taking a big one on the head while I was paddling out. The wave hit me so hard and square that it burst the zipper on my wetsuit open and pushed it to my ankles all in a split second. There I was writhing around on the bottom in all my glory with my wetsuit only staying with me as it couldn't get past the surfboard leash on my ankle. I was on my back on the reef; eyes wide open in panic with my contact lenses floating around my eyes. The waves were so big this day that no one was out except me and some of the locals stood on the shore watching as some ginger haired, sunburnt tourist went surfing. So, at this point I was well used to surfing bigger and bigger waves and facing the consequences that go with them. However, I knew that what I was planning on doing was going to be far and beyond anything I had ever experienced. I was going into the lions den so to speak. I was going to surf 'The Everest of Surfing'. As cheesy as that may sound, it is true, Mavericks is the Everest of our world and I was setting out on a pilgrimage with my friend Emmet to wait at base camp for four weeks for Mother Nature to allow us an opportunity to surf at one of the most infamous big wave surf spots on the planet.

It was December 19, 2003. Emmet and I were in Dublin airport. We had arrived with two massive board bags stuffed with 8 boards, wetsuits and then two ordinary luggage bags. I was so worried we would get to the check in desk and not be allowed on the flight. I had checked with the airline online and it said that one passenger was allowed one surfboard each which must not exceed 9'2" in length which is the normal length of an ordinary long board. Obviously they hadn't considered Mavericks surfer wannabes from Ireland when they were writing their rules. Our bags were 9'8" long and they each held four boards, and weighed an absolute tonne. It was such a mission getting them around. We ended up with two trolleys, one in front of the other and the boards placed flat across them both. We tried them sideways on the trolley and we were tripping people up and getting stuck in doorways and then we tried them on their ends but the door ways weren't tall enough. I was really stressing that they might not let us on the flight with them and then we would be in trouble! Somehow, we got them on, no questions asked, easy peezey! So easy I was constantly waiting for our names to be called over the speaker calling us to the desk to get them removed but it didn't happen. When you fly to the states and you have a connecting flight, you can't check your luggage straight through to the destination. You have to take your luggage off the flight and check it in again. This meant hauling the boards around Chicago airport. People would just stand and stare at us like we had two heads. One after another asking, "Is that a body?" or "is that the wing of the plane?" or "is it a canoe?" When they heard our accents and realised we were carrying surfboards people were astonished, I heard "they brought surfboards from Ireland" kind of echo along the queues of people as someone would whisper it to their friend and so on. It was the same when we landed in San Francisco.

We spent our first night in down town San Francisco when we arrived. The weather was pretty bad, torrential rain and windy. We slept like logs until 4am when the jet lag kicked in and we decided to wander into the city for a look around. There we where, two ejits walking around in the middle of the night on our own. We realised we had gone into a not so friendly neighbour hood when a car like you would see in a rap video cruised by really slow, all blacked out, we were sure we were about to get jumped. Coming from Northern Ireland you'd maybe think we were used to that sort of thing but we didn't really need that on the first day of the trip so we turned round and headed back towards the city centre. We ended up eating breakfast in a classic American diner. You know the ones I mean, all red and white decor, milkshakes and hash browns, that sort of place. It was called Loris, and we loved it, any chance we got, we went to Loris diner!

Emmet and I had booked a camper van or RV as they are known in the states. We figured that we would want to travel around a bit and a car was going to be a nightmare for all our boards. So we hired this 19footer, with its own shower and toilet, little kitchen and enough space to keep all the boards in too. It wasn't much smaller than my room at uni in Plymouth come to think of it! It was so cheap it cost us like $45 per day. This was way cheaper than getting a hotel room and a car and we could stay pretty much anywhere in it. Even the surfers we met were impressed with our ride and couldn't believe it cost so little, it was a real conversation starter at the beach!

We headed off on Highway One south bound. It was late afternoon, dark, still lashing with rain and you could have been forgiven for thinking we were still at home! We passed through Half Moon Bay on route to Santa Cruz to meet The Gerhardt's. Emmet had met a Californian long boarder in Bundoran who used to surf Mavericks but gave it up as he had his fair share of beatings and was content with giving Emmet the phone number for his friends Mike and Sarah Gerhardt to show us the ropes. The Gerhardt's are well known and respected big wave surfers. Emmet and I huddled into a payphone to shelter from the rain and called them. They invited us around to their house for dinner and told us we could stay as long as we wanted or at least park up out the front of their house. We eventually navigated our way through Santa Cruz and rolled up at their house and Mike ran out to greet us.

He's a big guy; he appeared to have muscles upon muscles. We went into the house and met Sarah. Sarah is what Emmet and I sort of expected in a California surfer. She is tall, blonde and athletic. They both looked very fit. They didn't look like average surfers, they looked like surfing athletes. We sat down to dinner and got talking about each other and we were really keen to hear all the stories about Mavs and they were keen to hear about our waves. To me this was cool as we were now in Santa Cruz, California, home to loads of the famous Mavericks surfers and we were eating dinner with two of them! Mike was telling us stories about surfing out there and some of the horror stories that go hand in hand with it. I was trying to find out as much as I could about Mavericks so that I could get a good feel for it in my head and almost have it visualised before I went out there.

To the best of my knowledge Waimea is where big wave surfing kind of started out. It is where big wave riding originated and most of the big wave surfers in the world will have surfed there. We hadn't surfed Waimea. I could tell Mike was a bit surprised that we were there to surf Mavericks yet we hadn't surfed Waimea first. I suppose he saw Waimea as a good experience gainer before anyone surfs Mavericks. We didn't have that notch yet and both Emmet and I began to wonder what we were getting ourselves into. One of the reasons I wanted to surf Mavericks was that the water was cold like home. I hated surfing in board shorts when I went abroad as I was so used to a full wetsuit and boots so it was one less thing to worry about. That might sound strange but I suppose it's whatever you are used too that makes you comfortable. They took us out the back of their house to a building Mike had purposely built to house all their guns. We were shown all their boards, it was amazing. They were telling us stories about waves they had ridden on particular boards and they mentioned that they may sell us a couple of them.

They gave us a tray of oat meal and raisin cookies that Sarah had baked for us and we went out and spent the night parked up outside their house. Emmet slept in the front of the van in a pull out double bed above the driving area and I slept at a lower level at the back of the van also on a double bed but I was able to hang my feet off the end there. Being 6'5" tall I always have to find beds that allow me to hang my feet over the end! We lay and talked about the last few hours and we were getting really excited. We were excited to be in Santa Cruz with the Gerhardts and everything was good! When we saw their boards we realised that we were going to need something bigger than what we had brought with us. Yeah we could definitely train and practice on the ones we had but we both agreed that we were going to have to get up first thing in the morning and start looking for suitable boards. We lay and talked for quite a while that night, I think we both couldn't believe we were actually there!

The swell was only small in the morning but Mike and Sarah took us out for a surf at a spot called Steamer Lane in Santa Cruz. I couldn't get my act together that morning and I was falling on all my waves, I'm sure Mike and Sarah were watching thinking I can't even stand up let alone try and surf Mavericks! We spoke to them about buying their boards and they said they would sell them to us but we went off to see their shaper Bob Pearson just to see what he had. His brand is Pearson Arrow and he makes a lot of boards for mavericks. We went into his store and there were guns and surf memorabilia everywhere. It was like being in a far off world to us. Bob wasn't around but we got to look at some boards anyway but realised that it was lucky Mike and Sarah would sell us two of theirs as these types of boards aren't just readily available in the shop. They need built specifically. I get all my boards' custom built for me but this would have taken a long time to organise in California.

Although it was flat, we couldn't resist a look at Mavericks. We needed to get it into our heads. We needed to see where it all happens and what it looked like first hand. As soon as we entered Half Moon Bay I began to see things I'd seen in videos and Magazines, I recognised the place though I'd never been there before! I saw the radio masts and transmitters on the headland and knew that was right in front of the break. We parked in the parking lot beside the harbour and walked round to the paddle out spot. It was so flat, sunny and still. Nothing like the menacing images we were used to seeing in videos. We went right down and stood on the reef, it was low tide so we could walk right out to the big rocks you always see in the foreground of the photos. I recognised one of the rocks in particular as there is a famous film sequence of a surfer on top of the rock and huge waves all around him. It was almost hard to believe that this beautiful place could produce the most evil waves on the planet. We walked around for an hour or so, while a few other tourists took photos of beautiful rock pools and starfish. I was picturing in my head the surfers I had seen in videos etc walking across this reef that I was standing on, I was seeing different clips of action in my head of them walking along the base of the cliffs with their guns about to paddle out. I just couldn't get my head around where exactly the wave broke. I knew it was in front of the rocks and I had a fair idea but with no swell on the reef I couldn't really see it if you know what I mean? It was a good exercise for us to go and check it all out. I suppose it is like a football match in a huge stadium, you would want to see where you are playing before the match kicks off so you can get a feel for the place. The only difference was, this wasn't like going into a game against human beings, this was like entering a gladiator's arena and having wild animals set upon you.

Over the next few days Emmet and I surfed a lot of the local breaks around the Santa Cruz area. Places like Steamer Lane and Scotts' Creek. We specifically surfed Scotts' Creek as much as possible as it always seemed bigger than other spots. Scotts' is a point break type of wave. If you're not a surfer you've probably just had a flashback of Keanu Reeves explaining to his boss that the reason he was late for work was because he caught his first tube that morning! A point break is how surfers describe waves when they roll in and break on a point of rock that sticks out into the ocean and then peel off along the point towards shore. A good example would be Jefferies' Bay in South Africa or Malibu in California. Scotts' is just north of Santa Cruz and because of the deep water channel beside the point, will allow surfers to ride pretty big waves. We got lucky with swell and Scotts' broke a couple of days in the triple over head range. We were able to surf the big boards we brought with us for Mavericks but we ended up breaking one. Emmet got caught inside by a set and the 8'6" he was on just broke in two when a wave hit him.

I remember very vividly being out at the point with Emmet just before dark one evening on our own with solid, triple overhead sets coming through. It was a dull overcast evening, not dissimilar to the weather at home in the winter. We were sitting out the back waiting on a set, just talking. I was facing out to sea and Emmet was turned more towards shore and the sandy coloured cliffs that disappeared up the coastline. I was talking about something when all of a sudden he looked over my shoulder, his eyes opened really wide like he had just seen a ghost. I said "What?" He paused for maybe a second or two and just before I was about to turn round to see what had just stolen his attention he screamed "SHARK!" I fired back "shut the f$&k up!" hoping he was taking the mickey but before I'd even finished saying it he was already prone on his board and scrambling for shore. We were maybe half a mile out to sea. I spun my board around and started to scramble with him. At this point I didn't know if the shark he'd seen was close by or in the distance or what, all I knew was to get ashore and not ask any questions. I was looking for a fin as my arms were going like windmills through the water.

I saw seals going airborne as they sprinted through the water on the inside section of the reef. They looked like they were running from something, I'm assuming the shark. I was so concerned about getting to the beach that in my moment of panic I'd somehow forgotten about the waves and out of nowhere both Emmet and I got taken out by a big wave that broke just behind us, knocking us of our boards. It hit me hard enough to pull the leash of my ankle and send my board to the beach without me. When I surfaced, Emmet and I looked at each other, both wide eyed and in shock that my board was gone. Then the seals surfaced right beside us and also looked at us wide eyed as if to say "what the hell are you doing here?" We crossed their path and that was frightening knowing what was coming behind them. Emmet told me to get on his board with him but I knew from rescuing people at home in the surf in the summer that getting someone on your board with you can make things difficult so I just started swimming for shore. The next wave took Emmet in and every time a wave hit me as I swam, I was spinning around under water thinking "oh f$&k, oh f$&k, oh f$&k!" I probably could have won the Olympics with that swim! As I got close to shore Emmet found my board and through it to me over the shore break and I made the last few strokes ashore on it. Exhausted we sat on the beach getting our breath back. Emmet had seen a fin swimming across the reef chasing the seals. Later that night we heard that a big great white apparently lives around that area of the coast!

Scott's was great; we had some good waves there. We also had a couple of good sessions at Ocean beach in San Francisco. It's a beach that also can produce some pretty big waves if the swell is right. Mike and Sarah had introduced us to lots of their friends and everywhere we went we were always greeted by someone who knew them and they would look out for us and make sure we had everything we needed. We spent New

Years' Eve with a lot of Mike and Sarah's friends too. We had been in California at this stage for nearly two weeks and although we had been having a great time and surfing loads we still hadn't had a Mavericks day yet. I was starting to get a bit anxious. I didn't want to run out of time and have to fly home without surfing there. It was my dream and I was determined to paddle into some big waves out there.

Mike had been watching a swell develop in the North Pacific and he was fairly sure that the next day was going to be our first chance to surf Mavericks. We had bought two boards from them. I took a 10'0 from Mike and Emmet a 10'4" of Sarah's'. We all went for a warm up that evening at another right hand point break to try out the boards. It is hard to test boards for big waves in small surf but it gave us a feel for them. That night was intense. I lay awake the whole night picturing what the next day was going to bring. I pictured what it would be like to catch the waves; I anticipated how scared I might be. I was really trying to visualise what it was going to be like based on what I had seen on videos, magazines and what Mike had been telling me. Mike, Emmet and I loaded the camper van with all Mikes' kit and we left Santa Cruz at 6:30am. Mikes' phone was ringing hot with people calling him trying to find out if he had seen the surf yet.

As we drove up the coast we saw Scott's Creek with waves breaking the whole way across the bay, closing out. It was obvious this surf was the biggest we had seen on our trip, so far. It took us an hour to drive to Half Moon Bay and the whole way up the coast we saw white water smashing up onto headlands. The air was cold and crisp, the sun was really bright and there was patchy fog. When we got there, the car park was packed full of vans and pickups with huge boards hanging out the back of them. There were loads of guys getting ready. We parked up and ran up the hill with Mike to take a look from the cliff. The eerie fog was made more intense with the sound of a fog horn resonating across the bay. When we got to the cliff edge we could just about see through the fog enough to make out a surfer dropping down the face of a huge wave way out at Mavericks. When the wave pitched out above him and then landed behind him, the explosion it made was incredible. We were standing at least a mile away yet the sound was amazing. It was obvious how much volume was in the wave. It was thick and heavy. I remember feeling excitement as I knew this was it, it was my dream to be here and surf these waves and I was about to do it! I also remember feeling nervous, and realising how serious this could be. I was frightened of getting hit by one of those waves. We went back to the car park and began to 'suit up'. We met a bunch of the crew as we waxed our boards. I always go quiet when I'm thinking or concentrating. Emmet was obviously nervous too and wouldn't stop talking. I actually put my headphones on as I didn't want to seem ignorant to him as I wasn't really listening to him chattering away. We started walking down the path towards the paddle out spot and I began to separate myself a little. I know that I need to focus and I find I sort of go into myself when I'm really focusing on something. The walk down the path takes about ten minutes. We walked along the edge of the still water behind the headland where we couldn't see the waves break. My mind was filled with thoughts. Should I really be doing this?, do I know what I've got myself into?, am I ready?, is Emmet ready?. None of us really said much as we walked. We got to the edge of the water, right behind the giant black rocks. The tide was higher than the last day we were there and the beautiful rock pools were now below water with a strong current flowing over them.

We set our boards down and did some stretching and warming up before we all waded into the water. Mavericks breaks behind the rocks so to get out there we paddled against the current along the back of the rocks until we got to the last rock, 'Mushroom Rock'. Once you get in line with that rock, it's time to start paddling out to sea. The waves at Mushroom Rock were about double overhead so we had to scramble our guns through them to get beyond the rocks and out into the deep water channel to start paddling to the peak of the wave. I got lucky and only took a few on the head, Mike got through just behind me and then Emmet a little later. As I was paddling out the sound of the waves was getting louder. It sounded like bombs were detonating out there. I was now out beyond the rocks. When I looked ashore I could see the huge radio masts commanding the headland behind me and the fog at the base of the hills. I was now on the surf side of the rocks and not the lagoon side so I could see the waves smashing over them. Although the surface of the sea was smooth and glassy, the heavy swell was rolling through and smashing on to the rocks after breaking on the reef out the back.

As I was paddling I passed another foreign surfer swimming with half of his board. He was clearly in shock. He was white with fear. He spoke in broken English but I gathered he had taken a beating in the impact zone and was heading in. As if I needed to see that! I continued to paddle out and after about 15 minutes reached the edge of the peak. There were a couple of guys out there already but I hadn't seen them ride a wave yet. I sat off to the side of the main peak in the safety of the deep water channel to watch the waves and get a feel for where I should be before going into the take off area. It felt like I was in the Monster Mavericks movie as I watched huge waves peak and throw out into huge tubes that I could see completely through. Mike showed us a line up marker he uses on the hill top to know where the main peak is. Being so far out at sea means it is difficult to know exactly what position you are in unless you have a point of reference. This marker really helped me as I knew where I should and shouldn't be.

Again, Mike was introducing us to all the guys and from time to time they would tell us to move a little as we were in a dangerous position if a set came through. They were all intrigued that we were from Ireland. I was really surprised when one of the guys, Matt, shouted out "don't worry about dropping in on a wave that we have already caught, just you guys go for it!" Normally surfers are very hostile and territorial but we were welcomed with open arms by these guys! It was a nice feeling as we felt enough pressure being out there in the first place without having to worry about locals being heavy with us! I remember my brother was interviewed by a television channel when he was 15 and they asked him about the territorial aspect to surfing. He explained it on national prime time television as being like a dog pissing on a lamp post, those words exactly. His English teacher wasn't too impressed that her pupil couldn't find a better way of explaining himself but it is a good comparison for a 15 year old to make! Surfing is renowned for having localism issues in various places. I haven't really had too many problems to be honest maybe because my brother and I have always been so big or maybe it's just because we show respect to local surfers. So many times I see surfers, in particular from home, going out at places and just surfing like it was their home break. It's so important to respect the people that surf these places on a daily basis and to let them have their pick of the waves and then if you are a visitor to take what is left. Anyway, the guys in the line up were very welcoming and I'm sure that was largely to do with Mike being with us.

I sat and watched waves breaking for about 45 minutes trying to suss out what was going on and where I did and did not want to be, before I paddled into the take off area. At Mavericks, there is a definite spot on the reef that the wave energy focuses onto. Mike's line up marker really helped me keep an eye on my position. The huge lines approach this particular spot on the reef ('The Main Bowl') and the wave bends and forms like a bowl or horseshoe type shape before the lip pitches out. The waves stack on the ledge of submerged rock like the reef is resisting them moving forward. It's like the wave is stopped in its tracks by the reef and is forced to grow taller and then when it has no where else to go its energy is forced to pour out from the top like a lip which falls into the trough or pit of the wave and explodes with immense force. There is a fine line between being in the right place to catch one and riding it and being in the wrong place and catching one on the head and it riding you!

I was definitely scared. I was paddling with jitters and butterflies in my tummy. I did not want to get caught out and take one of those huge waves on the head. I was being cautious. I tried to copy Mike as much as possible and stick to him. He was catching bombs out there and everyone was hooting him into them. It was obvious the amount of respect the others had for him. It was clear who the good guys were.

The confident seasoned surfers sat in the one spot and didn't flinch other than to turn round and catch a wave. They knew where to be sitting and when to move. I don't know if you can imagine what I was seeing out there but I'm trying to describe it in as much detail so you can at least get the feeling that I experienced on this day. There would be lulls between sets for maybe five minutes. When I saw a set coming, my first instinct was to paddle further out so that I wouldn't get caught in front of it with nowhere to run. The thing is, this would keep me out of danger but it wasn't going to help me catch some waves. I knew I had to stay put when a big set came through. Just stay in front of it and let it come towards me, then I needed to turn around and face the shore with my back to the wave, let it pick me up as I paddled and then ride it. This is a real psychological battle as it feels natural to paddle away from danger but if I wanted to ride one of these waves I had to be comfortable with putting myself close to the very spot in which it is going to break, turn around and then go on it. I was really struggling with it. Emmet didn't come into take off area for some time and watched the waves for longer than I did. The thing is, unless you sit on that particular mark up you will struggle to catch a wave out there. I tried to get onto them on the shoulder of the wave instead of fully committing to the main bowl but I wasn't getting waves. Emmet was watching me and although he wasn't speaking or shouting to me I could feel him willing me into them.

We spent 8 hours out there that first session and neither of us got a wave. We just couldn't get ourselves to commit to the main bowl and go on one purely because fear was taking over. Emmet ended up getting caught inside and taking a 30foot face on the head which sent him through the rocks. I was terrified for him. I remember seeing the first one hit him as I scrambled through mid-face and then when I surfaced seeing his board was completely gone as he was so deep under water that the board was also pulled down with him. I felt helpless as he got pounded just yards from me but he was ok in the end and somehow negotiated the rocks without a scratch. I ended up being out there as the last surfer in the water with Mike in the channel calling me in as it was getting dark. I was so angry with myself and determined to get one. It was so close to dark that the wave face was blackened out as the sun set behind the waves in the west. I eventually admitted defeat and began to paddle ashore. I was so annoyed with myself. I was really angry that I didn't have the balls to just go on one wave. I just wanted one wave but fear held me back. As we paddled in Mike reassured me that some people go out there numerous times before even catching a wave. I think I just felt the pressure a little more because I had travelled half way round the world and I knew I probably only had one chance at it and I had blown it for this trip. I was truly gutted.

When I got back to the car park everyone was laughing because Emmet had just done an interview to an American News Channel. The reporters seemed excited because an Irish surfer had come to surf Mavericks. Emmet gave them the Everest line and they loved it. It was broadcast later on the news as we sat in the nearby brewery talking about the session. As gutted as I was, I knew that although I hadn't caught a wave at Mavericks I was definitely one step closer to doing so!

The next day the swell had dropped but Scott's creek allowed us to surf some triple over head waves before we got lucky with Mavs again! As luck would have it we were going to get another chance to try and catch a few out there. The swell was slightly smaller than the first day but still some solid bombs were breaking. We knew we were lucky to score another day considering how rarely the swell is big enough for Mavericks to break. The water is so deep that waves don't show on the reef at Mavericks until they are big enough to feel the bottom and break, this only happens a handful of times in a season. We weren't going out there to not catch a wave this time! Emmet and I loaded the sleeves of our wetsuits with chocolate bars and then paddled out. We planned on an all day session again but didn't want to lose energy while we were out there.

Mostly the same crew of guys came out this time and a few others too. I ended up paddling for a couple right in position but fear held me back at the last minute despite everyone hooting me to go. This only added to my frustration. I knew I would eventually go on one but it needed to be the right one. All of a sudden I found the courage I needed, turned round and paddled into a decent one. It wasn't a bomb but was enough to warm up on although I fell at the bottom. The wave broke over me instead of hitting me and I just popped up. I got lucky and paddled back out right away. Next I was in line for a bomb. I knew I was in the right spot but a local guy Ryan screamed "Go!!!!!, you're in the slot!" That was enough to make me commit, I put my head down and stroked into the biggest wave of my life so far and stood up. The wind was howling up the face and trying to lift the nose of my 10'0" so I stomped my front foot down to keep it connected to the wave. I remember seeing the lip pitch out and land in the corner of my eye. I'd never seen a wave that big break so close to me, I made it to the bottom without getting bounced off and began to bottom turn. It was only then that I realised how big the wave actually was as I was able to look up at the wall as I put my board on a rail and pulled up the face before kicking out. I let out a really high pitched scream that was more likely to come from a girl's mouth than a man's. I was so stoked. I looked out to where Emmet was and he was sitting astride his board with both hands in the air screaming "YEEEEEOOOOOOOOO!" He was stoked for me! It was almost like that was all we needed to get us going.

We just needed one of us to ride one big one and make it and then we would find the confidence to ride more. Within about 5 minutes Emmet also rode his first proper one and we spent the afternoon catching waves with only a handful of other guys out. I was so relieved. All of a sudden the stress and pressure I was putting myself under was lifted and I was actually able to enjoy the experience of being out there. It was as if the first proper wave was enough to blow away some of the fear and allow me to take some chances and ride the waves I had dreamed about. Between waves, when I was paddling back out, I realised that I was living my dream. I was actually riding the waves I had dreamed of since I was 13. It was incredible.

I learned that fear and disbelief was really holding me back and that I was lucky to have another stab at it in the same trip. In saying that,

Mike and Sarah Gerhardt at home in Santa Cruz,California with their children Noah and Naomi.

Photo: Don Gerhardt

as determined as I was, it would have been foolish for me to paddle out there on my first day with little experience and paddle into the first bomb that came through. Fear controlled me but it probably held me back enough and allowed me to gain my bearings out there before actually committing and riding one. We had one more day of waves out there before we had to catch our plane home.

CHAPTER 5
project red

THE NORMALITY OF HOME began to fall into place in some ways. I was back into full swing with the business and glad to know that everything had gone according to plan and that nothing bad had happened while I was away. Mum was glad to see me back in one piece. I'm sure it was hard for Mum after losing her husband to then have her eldest son go to surf Mavericks. She was happy I had returned safe and in one piece.

Although normal life set in, I was already on my next mission. I wasn't content with doing a Mavericks trip once a year from now on. I knew those kind of waves existed off our shores but they just hadn't really been noticed yet. To the best of my knowledge, some guys like Willy Britton, Brian Tobin, Jonny Vance and American Mike Campbell and possibly a couple of others had already had a go at some of the more exposed spots but no one had really ridden anything jaw droopingly massive or if they had, they had kept it pretty quiet. I had heard stories of guys paddling out to various spots at size and managing to ride some waves. It was those guys who began to pioneer big wave surfing in Ireland. They saw bigger waves and they had the desire to ride them. They were no doubt held back by equipment limitations and were probably alone for the most part as they pushed themselves to surf bigger and more challenging waves for that time.

I was just back from Mavericks and my fire was fully raging. I just wanted to surf big waves all the time. I was extremely drawn to it and I loved being out in the sea when it was huge. I felt I had already surfed as big as I could on my local breaks and I knew that in order to ride waves similar to that of Mavericks, I needed to look further afield.

I bought some admiralty charts from a mapping shop in Bangor, Co. Down. I got the ones specific to the north coast right round to Bundoran. I knew that the waves at Mavericks happened because of an abrupt change in sea depth and a unique bottom contour causing already huge swells to grow even bigger. Without going into too much scientific detail and boring the hell out of you, this is because the waves come out of deep water and don't get slowed down too much by shallower water and the shape of the reef causes the waves to focus their energy on a particular spot of the reef causing them to grow bigger before breaking. This results in the waves keeping their size until they suddenly run into a rock ledge or reef underwater and are forced to break. So you end up with waves that are abnormally larger but also in some cases disproportionately more powerful and ferocious than normal.

I studied the charts very carefully and began circling areas of the ocean floor that looked to have a sudden change in depth or faced the right direction to pick up swell or that would hold wind etc... I searched the coast using these maps and also on foot. I circled lots of potential locations from as far east as Rathlin Island off the north coast and as far west as Sligo. I could have looked for other places but the search would be too thinly spread. I figured it best to focus on a fairly local area to begin with. I wasn't the first one to approach looking for big waves like this. In fact a project called 'The Billabong Odyssey' fronted by American Bill Sharp, had been doing this sort of thing since the late 90's and early 00's based in California. It was a project backed by international surf brand Billabong which resulted in the exploration of various coastlines and oceans around the world such as Chile, North America and Spain. The project brought together a crew of surfers and they attempted to find and ride big waves. They were successful in particular with a landmark session on a submerged sea mount 100 miles off the Californian coast at Cortez Banks. Billabong has since backed an annual global competition, 'The Billabong XXL'. Surfers and photographers who ride and photograph huge waves submit entries and if they are serious contenders they go into the competition for judging by a panel of surf media and big wave experts. Surfer and photographer teams are rewarded in cash for riding the biggest waves on the planet. The contest is very much the crème de la crème of big wave surfing and the awards show could be described as the Oscars of big wave riding. Most of the entries have come from the traditional big wave locations around the world mostly surfed by Hawaiians, Californians etc but a couple of Basque guys have also racked up a few entries whilst surfing a huge wave spot 'Belharra' off the Basque Coast. Nothing from Ireland had ever warranted being in the event to the best of my knowledge.

What I had begun to do here was not dissimilar to The Billabong Odyssey but on a more localised area. I didn't have any financial backing worth talking about which I might have regarded as a hindrance at the time but looking back it probably made me pretty resourceful. The problem was, some of these spots I had circled on my maps were miles offshore and I couldn't even see some of them from vantage points on land. I began to think about getting a boat to get out there. I checked lots of options and alternatives and finally got lucky as a family friend was actually selling one at the time. It was a 5.5m RIB (Rigid Inflatable Boat) with a 140hp engine on the back of her. She was called 'BOB' (Big Orange Boat). I didn't have the money to buy it at the time so he dropped the price a bit as long as Mum would buy it and I would pay her back monthly. I was earning money and didn't own a mortgage so I was able to meet the payments on it to keep the 'Boss' off my back.

Our family has a history of having boats around us, in fact I chose to name this book after one of them 'Mennie Waves'. I had been water skiing since the age of six behind our speed boat and Dad always had some sort of boat knocking around so I was already used to being at sea in boats never mind on a surfboard. This was quite a big financial commitment for me but that illustrates my passion and belief that these massive waves existed off our coast. I was so sure and passionate about it that I was prepared to buy a boat with borrowed money to go in search of them and ultimately ride them.

My friend Gareth 'G' Beckett was keen to be involved. I can't remember why Emmet didn't get really involved to be honest, maybe it was because the search was more focused in my neck of the woods, I can't honestly remember. Anyway, G was really keen on driving the boat. He didn't want to ride the waves; he just wanted to be involved from a planning, organising and driving point of view and to keep an eye on me. This was crucial as these waves I was in pursuit off, broke out at sea in cold water on submerged reefs. It was important to have someone with me.

We set out to various spots with Bob on our mission we called 'Project Red'. I could tell you about every spot in detail, the good ones and the bad ones but that would be another book in itself and it would blow the cover on some world class waves. We found five legitimate big wave spots and various other types of waves on our Project Red mission. I remember going to a harbour to launch one morning. We had identified three spots which are actually all within the same bay and we were going to check one out. I have been surfing a well known point beak inside this bay for years before but these spots only start to break when the swell is huge so normally you wouldn't even know these waves existed. We put Bob down the slip at this small harbour. The local fishermen all came over asking what we were doing as the swell was so big none of them could get out through the islands to fish. I didn't know where to start with our story. I mean, seriously, how do you explain to hardened fishermen that you are about to go out to sea in 30ft surf to ride waves a mile off the coast considering they don't even think getting out there is possible. I told them we were just going water skiing in the lagoon behind the islands and within seconds they left us alone. These spots are only accessible from a slip behind some islands and when the surf is huge, white water breaks all the way across the opening to the open sea so it is virtually impossible to get through unless you are lucky, mad or stupid or a mixture of both. I'm not sure which category we fitted into on this day.

I had adapted Bob to hold my guns down the side of the steering console so that they wouldn't bounce around. At this point this was probably the biggest surf I had seen at home and this was no doubt the biggest we had Bob in to date. We drove Bob through the lagoon and up to the point where a narrow pass is formed between the last island in the chain and the mainland. This pass isn't very wide and when you have 30ft waves breaking within half a mile of the other side it is complete chaos. We stopped in the lagoon just behind the pass. We could see huge peaks breaking on the reef beyond the pass. The only obstacle in the way was the pass itself and the huge lines of white water that were rushing through it. Bobs bow rocked in the rolling swell. Just in front of us the surf dissipated into deeper water so in effect there was a run of maybe 300yrds that we were stuck behind. If we could just get through it, we would be into the deep water channel next to the rock ledge that the big peaking waves were breaking on. I was sat behind 'G' holding onto his waist with our legs over the top of the boards strapped to the side of the console. I was cold already. To our right was main land, to our left was an island with some disused concrete buildings on it, behind us was the lagoon we just came across and in front of us was the doorway to the big waves I wanted to ride. We waited and watched the pass for about 20mins trying to see if there was anyway of getting through it. It was just constantly bottle necking more and more surges of white water through. I said "What do you reckon?" to which G responded "I reckon we just f£$%in gun it!" and as soon as he said it my weight was thrown backwards as he hit the throttle. I clung on tightly to his life vest and pulled myself back up on the seat. Bob started taking the white water head on as G blasted through the pass at speed.

We rounded the last corner and into the deep water channel. Now bear in mind this was our first time actually out at this location. I had seen it from land numerous times but never been actually out there. We all of a sudden where in a place we didn't know, swell was moving everywhere and we weren't sure exactly where was safe to be in the boat and where wasn't. We felt like sitting ducks. A big thick, slow moving set broke on the main peak so we knew right away where that was but we were unsure if there were actually any other places on the reef that waves were likely to just appear and break. I thought the safest place for me was to be in the water so I bailed and began to paddle over to the main peak while G kept Bob moving so as not to get caught out. I was more worried about Bob and G than actually catching a wave.

As sets came through I clawed my way over them as I tried to establish mark up points on the land like Mike had done at Mavericks. I kept finding myself out of position when a set came through. There was a very unsettled feel to the water and no real definition. I ended up too far north as a set came through but G was right where I needed to be. He was right on the peak of the wave. I thought it was lights out at this point as G drove Bob up the face of a wave that was about three times as big as the boat. I thought G was going to over power it and flip Bob off the back but he killed the throttle just as he got to the crest. Bob was vertical. G later said he was so vertical that he could see the engine at the back of the boat between his feet! Thankfully the wind was offshore and when Bob went off the back of the wave the wind blew him down flat again into the water. G looked at me from about 50yrds away and gave me the 'cut' signal as if to say that was too close, "This is chaotic lets get out of here". The thing was, it wasn't chaotic, it was just our first time checking it out and we hadn't fully got our bearings yet as the swell was so big. We needed a few more sessions out there before we would establish the safe areas for the boat and good mark ups for me so I could know where I needed to sit in order to catch the waves.

We tried out other spots too and we did score some good waves amongst all the chaos that comes with searching. I was scared because these waves hadn't been surfed before. I was worried that there may be a wreck or something on the reefs that I didn't know about. Our coastlines are scattered with wrecks from the Spanish Armada and also the world wars etc and I was worried that something could be on the reefs I was surfing that may hurt me if I get hit by a wave. Most of you are probably wondering why I didn't snorkel the reefs first. I don't know about you but I hate putting a snorkel on, I get that panicky feeling breathing through it and I hate to see what is down there to be honest. I'd rather let my mind make up its own underwater scenery than actually see rocks and seaweed with big fish coming out of caves and stuff! So, I had a thin impact vest made that I wore over my wetsuit when I was paddling. This gave me a bit more confidence. It was not unlike a water ski lifejacket but designed for protection rather than floatation. It was made with foam wrapped in neoprene but really thin unlike a lot of the others on the market for other water sports. I didn't want it to be too floaty that I couldn't get under the water if I had to swim under a wave.

Most surfers' ride waves at a beach that has been surfed for years and the fear of not knowing what is on the bottom probably doesn't enter the minds of the majority of people. I was way out at sea, in locations where I didn't know what was on the bottom, if there were wrecks or caves down there or anything. It was not a feeling that most surfers probably get and it definitely added to the fear factor. I remember the first time taking a big wave on the head, wearing the vest. It was at a spot I call 'Voices' because both Ben Granata and I heard voices out there despite being in the middle of nowhere. Ben is English and at the time worked as a photographer but as he had a power boat license he could drive Bob! He stepped in one day as G could only get one day off a week as he owned a shop so sometimes had difficulty getting away. This spot is an A Frame peak that heaves below sea level. By that I mean, it draws water so hard off the reef that the lip of the wave actually breaks below sea level. I had found it on the charts as it has a bathymetry with a sudden rise from 20m deep to 5m and then to 1.5m. It's the type of wave you can see through from one side to the other as the tube is so big and hollow. I had caught a few at this stage but nothing spectacular to be honest. I was feeling the fear for definite! I got caught inside by a big set and just managed to get under water as the lip threw over me; I remember hearing a huge 'WHOOOMP' as it smashed above me. All I could think about was my vest and hoping that if I'm going to hit something that it saves me. In the end I was ok but that was definitely the scariest moment I had so far whilst surfing these new spots.

I felt like I was feeling my way through big wave surfing at this stage, largely with a trial and error approach. It was a weird time in my life because I also felt like that in my every day life. I had taken on a completely new life within a short space of time and without a father there for advice and knowledge I was kind of feeling my way around in the dark. I found the business hard to get my head round at times as I didn't know what his plans were and what he was trying to achieve with various things so I had to kind of learn as I went along and let the experts who he had working for him just get on with what they were doing and then I could begin to piece together the whole jigsaw from looking in at it. Only now, looking back, do I realise that I was in a similar place with ordinary life as I was with my surfing. I didn't have anyone to really show me the way in my surfing at this point and so was taking calculated steps into my future based pretty much entirely upon my own judgement. This was also true of my life in general as now that my father was gone, the point of advice that I had always gone to was not there. I now had to think for myself and make decisions largely on my own. I don't mean to sound like I'm taking anything away from my Mum as that is not the case. Yes my Mum was there too but I'm sure you will agree that some thing's are Father questions and some our Mother questions. I was lucky to have a strong group of people around Mum and I who knew what the score was and who were able to look after things for us. I was also lucky to have a good solid group of friends around me who supported me and tried to help me in various ways and not just in my surfing. I was constantly worried about Andrew who was back at university in Plymouth and although he wasn't involved with what was going on at home, and that might have appeared better, he didn't have the direct support from all his oldest friends and Mum and I. It was definitely a very intense time in all of our lives.

Right: 'Lords' a spot I found during Project Red situated in some of the most treacherous waters in the country. This location has sunk boats and scuba divers have disappeared out there.

AT THIS STAGE I had found a number of big wave spots. I had surfed some of them and I scoped out the rest. I had definitely surfed the biggest waves I had ever surfed in my home country and that was down to a number of things but mainly having a boat to get to them. I had made notes and scribbled all over the admiralty charts to remind myself which spots worked in what conditions etc. I had located access points to all the waves and escape routes should something go wrong. I began to feel that I had a good range of surf spots up my sleeve. Various British magazines told me that if I got photographs from theses spots that they would be really keen to run them in their magazines. I thought if they wanted photographs they would have sent someone over but maybe they didn't want to commit financially to something they hadn't seen any proof off.

I had Bob for about 12 months when I decided I would go to Todos Santos is Baja, Mexico over the New Year period of 2004/2005. Todos Santos is one of the handful of big wave surf spots that is known and recognised globally. It breaks off an island 12 miles out to sea. Some of the most terrifying photographs I have ever seen have come from there. There is one really famous one a surfer almost airborne dropping down the face of this monstrous wave during a surf contest there. I used to stare at that poster all the time just wondering how on earth he managed to catch that thing and how he didn't fall as the wave looked so steep. He was no doubt on a 9 or 10 foot board but this photograph in particular made even that look small. It was a very inspirational photograph for me and I wanted to go to Todos to see if I too could ride a wave like that.

I now had a lot more experience under my belt that I didn't before my first Mavericks trip and I felt a lot more capable to catch and ride big waves. You may be wondering why I was going abroad again to surf big waves whenever I have just found them on my doorstep. Well it's like any sport if you are amongst good sportsmen in whatever the sport may be, you will progress. I knew that from my experiences in England and surfing in other countries around the globe. If I was surrounded by good surfers my performance level grew. So, I knew that by going to another big wave spot I would gain from the experience and be able to bring that knowledge home and apply it to the waves I had at home.

Emmet couldn't make this trip as he had important things he needed to do at home so I went alone without my Mavericks buddy. This was a bit strange for me as I liked having him with me but I was also sort of getting used to following my dream on my own. I landed in Los Angeles with my guns and hired my own campervan, this time a little smaller. My plan was to wait around the San Diego area next to the border and as soon as the chart looked like Todos would break, I would drive straight there. I waited for 2 weeks and the surf stayed small. One day I surfed the pier at San Clemente when it was howling onshore and I broke my only short board I had on the trip. I bring a short board so that I can surf every day and then if it gets big I have all my guns there. The waves had been small for two weeks and when I broke my short board I was getting strung out. I had been parking up every night between two parked cars on the edge of a dual carriageway as I kept getting moved on by the police. I learned that if I parked in a street with other cars the cops must have thought the campervan was just parked there and probably assumed no one would be stupid enough to sleep there. They didn't bother me after that. I got a call from a guy I knew from laguna beach who said there was a potential Mavericks swell for first thing in the morning. He couldn't make it as he was about to go on holiday but he rang to let me know as he was aware I was hanging around with not much to do.

I had walked the pier at San Clemente about 100 times each night, I had eaten in every café and restaurant to try and keep my mind occupied. As soon as he called me, I loaded the van with gas and blasted into the 9 hour drive to Mavericks through torrential rain. I don't know if you have ever driven in the states but as you come past Los Angeles you come to this section of road that has about 9 lanes going in each direction. In Northern

Ireland the most we have is about 4 lanes coming out of Belfast for about a mile so this was scary as f%^k! There I was in my campervan looking like a proper tourist driving through, pissing down rain as all the LA workers appeared to be heading home after a hard day at the office. It was chaos; cars were flying past me on both sides at high speed. Also the roads there are concrete and there are joints in the road to stop the concrete cracking so every time the van or another car went over the joints there was a thud which added to the stress! It's a pretty hectic experience!

Anyway, I arrived in Half Moon Bay at 3am and parked up between two fishing boats that were out of the water and parked on the roadside. I was on the cliff top at 6am, alone. No pick ups with big boards hanging out the back, no other surfers around, just silence broken by the fog horn every now and again. Yes there was swell but not like the first time Emmet and I saw it early in the morning. The swell wasn't big enough this time, it was humping up on the reef as it passed through but wasn't feeling the bottom enough to break. Every now and again a wave would just topple over and cap on the reef. It wasn't doing it! The nine hour drive consisted of my head being fully amped and pumped for Mavericks, I was on a mission and I couldn't wait. I was so concerned about making it before it got bright that I didn't even want to stop to take a pee and instead filled up a couple of empty energy drink bottles! As I stood there peering into the foggy darkness someone appeared behind me and said "Is it breaking?" I turned round and replied "Not really". I realised that the guy was someone Mike introduced me to but I couldn't remember his name. We watched for a little longer before he took off and headed home leaving me standing on my own again, willing the sets to get bigger and allow me to get out there. It didn't happen and I ended up heading north to Ocean Beach and surfing some pretty sizey waves there. It wasn't Mavericks but I was glad to eventually get in the water on my 8'6". This turned out to be my only decent surf of the three week trip and I ended up flying home without scoring either Todos or Mavericks. It was a pretty lonely trip to be honest and I was glad to get home at the end of it.

beyond humanly possible

WHILE I WAS AWAY I had been pondering the idea of Tow In Surfing (see glossary of terms). I knew there was serious potential to ride waves at home that were bigger than any seasoned big wave surfer at that time thought humanly catchable by paddle arm power alone. There is only so fast someone can paddle a big board to match the speed of a big wave. I knew that I needed to be considering Tow Surfing as an option if I wanted to continue to surf bigger and bigger waves. I had been paddling into big waves for some time now and yes I could have focused my efforts on being able to master that alone and hone my skills on that but my objective was to ride the biggest waves I possibly could and I know as well as most big wave riders know that there is a limit to what is catchable by just using arm power to get into the waves.

Tow In Surfing started in Hawaii, as did big wave riding, as far as I'm aware. The guys out there were using the method to catch waves bigger than people had previously ridden by paddling in. I'm not 100% sure who started it as with everything, I think there a number of people claiming to have been the first and I don't want to get it wrong and annoy anyone. Who did it first didn't matter to me though, I was only concerned with was it something I should be doing. Now if you are not a surfer and you are reading this you have probably just asked yourself "Why on earth would someone want to surf a wave that they couldn't catch on their own?" You might also be thinking that if it isn't possible to catch those waves on your own then they should be left unridden and that should be the limit to what surfers can ride.

Unfortunately or fortunately depending upon your stand point, like anything, there are always extremists in every walk of life. For example climbers could be content with standing at the base of a climbing wall in the local leisure centre and instructing people on how to climb to the top of their 20 foot wall or they could take it upon themselves to climb the biggest mountain in the world. This is what I'm trying to explain to you. People who climb Everest are pushing the limits of human endurance and boundaries every time they attempt it. That is exactly what big wave riding is to surfing. It is the far extreme of the sport and for that reason only a small percentage of people will ever have the desire to chase down and ride the biggest waves they can find. Like my example with the climbers, I could decide that I want to spend my time teaching people to stand up on a foam board at my local beach and I could spend my days surfing the local beaches quite contently. Or I could choose to take my surfing and surfing in general to new levels. Maybe someday I will own a surf school and teach people to surf but that has never really been anything I've passionately wanted to pursue so far. I chose to push my ability in surfing and personal boundaries to new heights through riding waves as big as I could find. In order to do that, I first had to sacrifice Bob.

Yes, I finally decided to trade Bob for a PWC (jet ski / ski). Bob had served me well but I knew that in order to ride the biggest waves I could find, I needed to have the availability of a ski. It would have been brilliant to have been able to afford to have both but that wasn't an option. I wasn't made of money and I had no financial support from my sponsors. I fully committed and invested in this by myself.

The biggest problem I saw in Tow In Surfing was that it appeared to be a different sport to surfing for a number of reasons. It involved the use of a PWC (Personal Water Craft) or jet ski as they are more commonly known. It also involved a team work situation and that is something surfers aren't used to. Surfing is a solitary activity. You have a surfboard, you paddle out and you catch waves. When it's big and there are a few guys in the water people do look out for each other but you are still largely on your own. I had been more or less completely on my own so far. G and Ben were involved with Project Red which was a team effort but that was it. I didn't have any experience working extremely closely with another surfer in order to ride massive waves.

I got hold of a bunch of dvds of tow surfing at spots like Mavericks and Jaws and I studied them closely. I worked out what was going on and what equipment I needed. I could see that this wasn't just going to be expensive in the form of buying a ski but there are so many accessories that go with it that I needed to get too.

I could see from the DVDs that all the skis were using rescue sleds on the back of them like lifeguards have. This was to make pick ups of fallen surfers quick and safe to do. I did some research on the net and found out that they cost in excess of $1200! I couldn't believe that bit of foam like an over sized boogie board would cost that much! I asked Circle one if they would make me one and they said they would but there were lots of manufacturing complications that ended up in me never getting one from them in the end.

I was able to see that a lot of the guys in Hawaii and California were using Yamaha skis so I sourced the main dealer in Northern Ireland and went to check them out. All I knew about jet skis was that they were generally owned by people that just raked them round as fast as possible through tourists and generally caused a lot of annoyance. I didn't want to appear like that. I explained to the guys what I wanted to do. It's always hard trying to explain to someone who has no clue what you are talking about. They kind of look at you like you are talking crap! "Aye 30ft waves in Ireland mate? Aye dead on, what drugs are you taking?" That was the general consensus so I always tried to leave out the bit about the big waves when talking to people about surfing. These guys though had just sold a ski to another couple of guys who were also looking at riding some big waves. I was like "Really? Who?" He opened his file and read out the name "Lahinch Surf School, does that mean anything to you?" I knew right away it was two guys I knew from Tramore, Waterford. John McCarthy owned Lahinch Surf School and his mate Dave Blount spent a lot of time there but worked in Dublin. It was a surprise that they had come up to buy a ski but at the same time it made me feel like someone else could see the potential too! Both John and Dave have spent time in Hawaii and surfed their fair share of big waves out there. They are older than me; maybe five to ten years older, I'm not honestly sure. They had been scoping out this spot in Co. Clare at the time which was rumoured to have big waves. I suppose they where thinking along the same lines as me in that they wanted to be able to tow into waves there as they thought it had potential to create waves bigger than paddleable.

I drove home with my new ski on the tow hitch. I felt like a right tosser driving through the towns with this big shinny jet ski on the back. It felt like everyone was looking at me probably thinking "look at him; he thinks he's pretty cool!" Thing was, I was more embarrassed than they could imagine.

Word started to spread that Meenie has got a ski. (For some reason loads of people pronounce my name Meenie. They spell it wrongly and they pronounce it wrongly). Anyway, word was out and I was getting asked all sorts of things. People still had no idea that huge waves existed and didn't believe it. At this time, there still had been no really big waves being ridden and captured on camera, well nothing bigger than what was considered paddleable at that time anyway. Surfing was just starting to be recognised by people in Northern Ireland as possible here and they weren't in any way ready to believe that not only are there two foot white water waves at Portrush but in actual fact there are 40foot waves not that far away, in the right conditions. So maybe you can understand how mad I must have seemed. People probably saw me as a bit optimistic to say the least. The local surfers knew there were big waves out there but I don't think anyone expected the story that was about to unfold.

My friend Richie Fitzgerald had a ski in Bundoran. He and his English friend Gabe Davies had one. They had ridden a couple of sizey swells with it. They obviously saw potential too and wanted to try and harness that. They, like me, saw that paddling into these waves was probably not going to be possible when the seas got huge. So, you can see now that there were a few of us spread out across the island who were all starting to see the potential to ride huge waves here in Ireland all around the same sort of time. Dave and John had the bottom of the country covered, Richie had Bundoran covered and I had the North and North West covered. I later discovered that another crew in Englishman Mikee Hamilton, Aussie Paul O'Kane and their friend Dave Lavelle had also been dabbling with tow surfing too around the Easkey area of Sligo. Between us, we were all, unknowingly to one another, in search of a similar thing; we all wanted to ride big waves!

I spoke to Ritchie and we agreed to give it a go together and try and ride some big waves. I was excited about this as he had already been doing it for a while with Gabe so could probably teach me some stuff...

With Ritchie in Bundoran and me in Castlerock, we were two hours apart and this caused problems because if we wanted to practice together one of us had to drive a full four hour round trip. I couldn't do that every other week, that wasn't enough. I started looking for someone locally to help me out. I needed a partner, someone who was capable firstly at surfing but also someone who had already gained experience in big surf. If there is someone in this country who rides legitimate big waves, I'm pretty sure I know them personally or at least know of them. I was fairly sure that no one in Northern Ireland was going to be of the calibre I needed to find although I needed to start somewhere. Emmet was the obvious candidate but he was also in Bundoran and I needed to be practicing at least two or three times a week. G was so busy with his shop that he couldn't commit any more time to it. I needed a surfer, a good surfer with good ocean knowledge and experience. I just couldn't think of anyone to be honest. The most rounded surfer we had was my brother but he was in Plymouth and I knew better than to ask him as big waves weren't his thing. Andy Hill is a well known surfer who owns a surf shop but I knew that although he had the outstanding surfing ability, he didn't have the same desire as me to ride huge waves. I needed someone just like me really, someone, with a raging passion, to surf bigger and bigger waves. In fact Andy had recently got into photography and one day by chance took a few shots of me riding waves at East Strand which actually won us 'The Mananan Big Wave Competition'! The Mananan was a photo competition (similar to 'The Billabong Odyssey' but on a local level as opposed to global) where the images or video captured of surfers were judged. The winner would be the surfer and photographer who had captured and ridden the biggest wave of the year in Irish waters. We didn't set out to do this, it just so happened that East Strand was at its biggest and cleanest in years, I was out there and Andy pulled into the car park just in time to shoot me catching a couple before dark.

The winning wave was about 15 feet on the face and at the time was considered a big wave in Irish surfing by most people's standards except for a small handful of clued in surfers. People were constantly commenting on how big it was and seemed genuinely blown away that it was actually East Strand. I knew waves, a great deal bigger than that existed and the fact that people were so gobsmacked at that wave made me realise that they were going to be in for a shock when they see what really is out there. At this stage it seemed literally only a few of us who realised that it was possible that within the next few years some of us would be riding waves as big as the famous big waves of Hawaii or Mavericks. I needed a tow partner!

I knew from my own experience so far that there are only a very small handful of people with the passion to ride big waves, across the globe, let alone in Northern Ireland. I thought about the guys at Mavs and Jaws. They were local guys to their area but they all had big wave experience before they started towing. They knew what it was to get beaten out there as they had already been paddling into big waves. To my knowledge, I was the only Northern Irish surfer doing this and one of maybe two or three guys on the whole island so I was going to struggle to get someone locally who would be up for it and up to it. I began to think would I be better forgetting about the tow in thing and stick to paddling rather than start tow surfing with the wrong person and end up getting into trouble or hurt?

I knew this wasn't the answer. Let's face it, I had a new toy and I wanted to play! Imagine getting a new toy at Christmas and not playing with it right away! I began to use the ski with my friends at the local beaches. Everyone loved messing around and before long; most of us were capable of being towed on the rope.

My closest friend at the time was Barry Johnston or Baz as I called him. He was a big lad. I have heard people refer to Baz as "Being well made". He is a 6 footer with reddy blonde hair, built like an ox and could lift anything. You know the kind of guy I mean, big and strong. He was just as used to carrying bags of cement around as a surfboard and that was obvious from the way he lugged his battered 6'8" around with him. Baz would do anything for me. He is a great guy. He helped me out loads when Dad died especially with practical hands on stuff that I was useless with. Baz tried to help me with the tow in stuff at the start and drove the ski a couple of times for me but we weren't able to get it to work. It was annoying because he would do anything for me and we got on really well.

I met a guy called Carl Russell shortly after Dad died. I had got to know him gradually over time.

Carl originally came from Jordanstown, Co. Down. He was very sporty and took part in pole vaulting, athletics and other sports as well as surfing. He wasn't solely into one sport and did a bit of each from what I gathered at the time. He was really into his training for sport. We started doing a bit of training together with the objective that we would make a tow team and have a proper go at it. I knew from the outset that Carl was used to putting a lot of time into training for various sports and he did the same with this. We started doing weight training and cardio exercises in his garage in Bushmills. I too have been very into my training. I have done a lot of weight training and swimming over the years particularly to do with surfing. It was cool to have a training partner as I was used to always doing stuff on my own and having him to train with made me have to do it and not make any excuses.

We started taking the ski out in big surf at Portballintrae. Portballintrae is a beautiful beach with the stunning back drop of an old state building on the headland. It is so picturesque. The River Bush runs out there. The River Bush is the river used by The Bushmills Whiskey Distillery just up stream. The water is always an auburn colour as the river bed is peat based so it always has a stained appearance.

The North coast is more or less a no go area for jet skis. People hate them so much that they have been banned from most beaches except a couple. This meant we had to launch it at places that were no where near where we wanted to go and then drive it there along the coast. The thing is, jet skis are usually associated with people who use it twice a

This is me in a frothy keg of my own whilst surfing in the mouth of the river bush, Portballintrae. A couple of miles upstream kegs full of the famous Bushmills Whiskey are being brewed.

year and have had no training or ocean experience before hand so I can understand people's hatred for them.

Portballintrae is one of those places surfers go when the surf is small as it faces west and picks up lots of swell from the North Atlantic. It is the most exposed beach on the coast. Once it gets to slightly over head high most people opt to surf somewhere else as the waves can get quite challenging. If you have ever been to Hossegor in France and seen some

of the waves there you will have an idea of the kind of surf Portballintrae can produce. It can be really heavy at times there. The waves break in quite shallow water on shifting sandbanks. The waves draw so hard off the bottom at times that sand is actually lifted off the sea bed by the waves making them appear brown in colour. The thing is that because it is so exposed not only does it have the biggest waves when the swell is small, but it also has the biggest waves any day of the year. So...when the whole coast is getting pounded and we needed somewhere to practice driving etc, Portballintrae was a perfect choice. I figured, if you could drive a ski there on a solid 3-4 times over head stormy day and be able to get in and out from the beach then that would be pretty good experience to have for when it's really big at one of the reefs.

We put in a fair bit of time at Portballintrae on the ski. We practiced towing each other and picking each other up. I hadn't got a rescue sled or a tow board at this stage so we were hindered by equipment. I tried to make a sled out of an old knee board that Dad had bought me for my 8th birthday when I was water skiing. The knee board didn't work at all and it was actually dangerous to be honest.

It took us quite a while to get the hang of things and work out what to do. One of the main things we worked on was to time driving the ski with the waves so that the surfer would get put onto the wave at the right time near the top and not leave either of us too low on the wave to get clobbered with no speed. Some days were really stormy and bumpy. It really hurt my back hanging onto a rope and being towed through two foot surface chop. We found it difficult to get the right balance of driving the ski at a speed that we could handle the chop but also at a speed which the surfer could comfortably stay on his feet while holding the rope without falling backwards or without being pulled forwards and off the board!

The ski has a tendency to come out of the water when it hits chop and when that happens the rope slackens a little bit, and then when the ski connects with the surface again if you are hanging onto the rope, you nearly have both arms pulled out of their sockets as the slack in the rope

Carl and I, North Coast, 2005.

is sharply straightened out. It was hard to learn to drive at a constant steady speed, keeping the hull of the ski in the water as much as possible so as to keep the surfer on his feet. It was frustrating for us both trying to learn as we went along. I knew that doing this at a beach break were the waves were coming from all directions, would prepare me for more forgiving situations at reefs.

If you're not a surfer that might not make sense, in fact you may be completely lost at this stage but I am trying to explain things in as much detail as I can. A beach break is what we call waves that break on sand bars. The waves generally shift around a fair bit and never really break in the same place. This made driving the ski like dodging bullets at times as we had to be really on the ball or we could get knocked off the ski. At a reef break, the waves break on rock ledges or boulders and usually have a deep water channel beside the reef. This means that the waves mechanically break on the rock ledge or boulders making them more predictable. Yes, it is a lot more dangerous especially with the kind of waves I was after but it is also safer too as surfers can get to know the characteristics of a spot, its moods, the type of waves that it will have in a particular swell etc. That might sound daft to you if you aren't a competent surfer but it's true, you do become acquainted to surf spots and you know them and how they will react in a range of conditions.

I've heard people say I appear very calm when they meet me but the truth is far from that. I am highly strung and extremely impatient. I want everything done yesterday. I hate being late, I like everything on time and I don't like to miss a beat. I am a nightmare to get on with especially when the surf is huge and I want to be there ready for first light. I know how quickly the big swells arrive and how quickly they go. I know there is no time to waste but no one seems to understand that I want to be wherever it is going to be biggest before first light. The window for being out there is small as the storms we have are so close to shore that the winds come with the swells meaning if you want to ride big waves when the surface is clean and not choppy then you might literally only have a few hours in order to do it. In some other locations across the globe, the swells come from weather systems which are further out to sea and therefore the winds can often be lighter and the swell can last longer because the wind isn't blowing it to pieces. This means that there can literally be only a few hours in a day where big waves can be rideable here.

Carl and I started trying to ride bigger waves together. I took him to 'Voices' one morning. Well, actually we left at 3am to be there for first light. 'Voices' wasn't getting the swell as the direction of the swell was meaning it was going straight past the bay. Let me explain...The swells we get come off low pressure systems out at sea. The position of that low pressure system dictates the direction from which the swell is coming from and from that surfers can tell which spots will receive the most swell depending on the direction. 'Voices' needs a North West or North Swell for it to get full exposure to the swell. This swell was only west so it was going past the mouth of the bay and hitting some other more westerly facing spots along the coast. We launched and headed along the coast to try out a couple of those spots.

This session made us realise that the very second you look at the jet ski, things start going wrong or maybe a more positive phrase is 'things become more challenging!'. This session turned into us running over the jet ski rope which made it get sucked up into the impeller and rendered the ski unusable. We had to swim the ski through triple over head surf for about 3/4s of a mile, unscrew the bottom plate, cut out the rope, then screw it back together again all on a rocky shore line. Then we got the trailer stuck in the sand trying to get it out with the van and some wee old woman had to come down and role her trouser legs up to help us! Imagine us two young fit guys totally exhausted needing an elderly woman to help us. I was in the van reversing down the beach, Carl was standing in the water leaning on the trailer using his weight to move it as he was too tired to push it anymore and between us was this pensioner with her trousers rolled up pulling the trailer out of the sand on her own. As embarrassing as it was, neither of us refused her help! I signed the old lady up as our new tow partner and the three of us lived happily ever after, THE END. No, seriously, I was starting to realise that this was nothing like surfing, this was completely different! I had never had anything like that happen in ordinary surfing or even paddling big days or even with Bob. This was a whole different ball game! It felt like every time we got over one problem, the next one was just about to happen.

The next thing I needed was a tow board. I didn't know what I needed to order for tow surfing. I knew it would depend on the types of waves etc but I wasn't sure exactly what to get. I started searching the web for people to ask. I knew that getting someone my size who tow surfed was going to be difficult to find and to ask advice of. I eventually came across an interview with a guy called Chuck Patterson on www. towsurfer.com. He looked like a super hero, massive bulging muscles.

He didn't look as tall as me from the photos on the site but he looked so well built that his weight would at least match mine if not exceed it. I emailed Eric Akiskalian who owned the site to ask him for advice based on the fact I had just seen photos of this super hero figure. I told him my stats, the types of waves we have here etc and asked for his advice on what I should get built. He replied with literally this. "Try 5'10" or 6'0" x 16.5" x 2". That was it, nothing more. I thought about it for a bit and was going to ask for more information but in the end I didn't. I thought that tow surfing is very young and not much research had been done on equipment so I emailed the dimensions to Circle One, asked them to triple glass it for more weight and that was it. Most surfboards are preferred light so that they can be moved around on the wave easily although with tow surfing we are dealing with much more speed and surface bump so if they are heavy they handle the speed and the bumps much more easily. When the board arrived I actually cut a hole in it and got a role of lead from the building site and fitted another 5kgs of weight into the deck to weight it even more. I think it was about 8 or 9 kgs by the time I had re-glassed the hole in it. I also inserted foot straps into the deck. This is also completely different to ordinary surfing. There is no way an ordinary surfboard would have straps on it. They aren't needed and also they would get in the way when lying on the board to paddle it. I had to work out the position for them on the deck so I placed another board beside the new board and transferred my normal stance onto the new one based on where the wax on the old board had been squashed by my feet. I then moved the front foot placement a little further forward than normal so that I would be sure to have a solid, wide stance. This stance is sometimes referred to as 'Survival Stance' or in fact 'Poo Stance!' I'm sure I don't need to explain that one now do I? It basically is a wider stance than normal as the objective is to stay on your feet!

So there I was armed with a new weapon, something which to most people would look ridiculous but to me seemed normal as all the other guys towing in were using them and that meant I needed one too. I stand with my left foot forward and Carl stands with his right foot forward. This meant he wouldn't fit the straps on the board so was going to have to get one of his own if he wanted to tow. Previous to me getting that one from Circle One, Baz and I tried to make one from an old board. Baz got the angle grinder out, cut a hole in an old short board about 8" x 10", filled it with a block of wood, some steel angled fittings and resin and glassed it back up again before spraying it black to conceal the mess! I don't know what we were thinking, there was metal and glass fibre sticking out of it with two lengths of roof rack tie downs wrapped in piping insulation for foot straps!

So I had one board, a ski, no rescue sled and a crappy 'dental floss' style water ski rope but despite not having all the top notch gear, I was determined to make do with what I had and get onto some big waves.

While I was trying to get it together up north, John and Dave were doing the same thing down in Clare. Photos appeared of them riding this perfect, glassy big wave spot beneath the Towering Cliffs of Moher. It didn't look like Ireland. It looked like Hawaii. The water was blue and the sun was shinning. It was hard to believe. The waves were so perfectly formed, not the raging swells that are normally associated with Irish waters. They had come across this wave beneath the cliffs and they started towing it. As I said before, I'm not going to state who was the first to surf there as again I don't know the facts 100% but to the best of my knowledge they were the first. The spot was soon given the name 'Aileens' after the headland beneath where it breaks.

I was stoked for them to be doing that, their dreams were obviously coming true and they must have loved it. I was also a little frustrated that I hadn't got to that stage with tow surfing yet. Maybe I was spending too much time on training and preparation and not enough time just doing it? I wasn't sure. All I knew was I had to get things moving as I didn't want another big swell to go by without the opportunity to tow surf if conditions were right.

Over the next few months there wasn't much swell to be honest. I remember going out once or twice with Carl but we still hadn't gone out in anything really big. I had given Carl an old 7'2" of mine which was good for paddling reefs as he didn't have a board for that but I didn't have a tow board I could give him.

I phoned my mate Andrew 'Cotty' Cotton. I met Cotty through a company called Gulf Stream who used to sponsor my brother and I with boards. They were from Croyde Devon. Cotty glassed and shaped boards there. I had seen him only recently in Sri Lanka at a contest. We had both been doing the BPSA Tour and the top 16 surfers were invited to compete at a final event in Sri Lanka. While we were there I had been telling Cotty about the big waves at home and he was keen to come over at some stage though to be honest he had been saying that for years but always opted for somewhere warmer and cheaper, and who could blame him. I knew he had been to Hawaii and surfed Waimea (The wave Mike Gerhardt had thought Emmet and I might have surfed before we went to Mavericks). He was keen on big wave surfing and was a good surfer.

As luck would have it, Cotty was just about to book flights to Madeira to go out and spend a few weeks with big wave surfer Ralph Freeman and his partner Shay. I was considering going on another Mavericks trip at the time but again no one was up for it so when Cotty suggested I should go to Madeira too, I jumped at the chance and booked my flights that day to fly out in a few weeks time.

the test

CARL AND I WERE still a team. We weren't getting any big surf really and the equipment issues weren't getting any better.

A big swell was forecast for Bundoran, Co. Donegal. I know Bundoran well, I've been surfing there for years at all the spots. This swell was looking good and a few of us headed down to Bundoran for a couple of days. I brought the ski only in case we could get a chance to surf Mullaghmore Head. Mullaghmore is renowned as a big wave spot. That is where Ritchie and Gabe had towed a few times in their early days. As luck would have it the swell was huge.

On the second day of the trip, I went out to take a look at Mullaghmore with Carl and it was amazing. Huge walls of water were standing up on the rock ledge off the coast and exploding with force and then peeling along the ledge before dissipating into the deep water channel. We were parked on a hill facing down the point and out to sea watching the waves march in. The entire headland is so exposed it has no trees or plants on it except a few lonely palms! I don't know what they are doing there but they seem to like the view!

I had my paddle guns in the van with me and the ski on the back. I sat in the van watching the waves with my friend Mark Miller and Carl. Mark is my friend from Coleraine, he isn't into big waves but loves surfing and was really keen to watch from the headland. I was frothing to get out there. I was so amped. It looked like the big set waves were about 30 foot on the face, thick with water and very powerful. I had two options; I could paddle or use this as a practice tow session. I had all my big wave boards with me and the ski so I could at least paddle. I remember feeling scared; I think you would need to be crazy to not be frightened about the prospect of paddling out there. Even Emmet has never been in the water at Mullaghmore. That's how scary it is! He would rather go and surf Mavericks in California, than attempt to ride Mullaghmore, in his own back garden: that says it all!

About 30 minutes went by and we were still sitting in the van. I was starting to get myself ready to jump in off the headland and paddle out on my own but Carl said he would try and tow me into one on the tow board if I wanted too. He didn't want to ride one himself but was prepared to give driving me a go. I had told Carl that he didn't have to do it if he didn't want to as I was more than willing to paddle out on my own and just paddle into them and if I got a few then I'd be happy enough but in the end we drove round to the harbour and put the ski in. There were a lot of nerves around that was for sure. Just before we saddled up and headed out, Carl shook my hand as if to say "Let's do it!" Out we went around the harbour and then drove out to the point which is about a five minute ski ride.

Carl and I before towing Mullaghmore for the first time.
Photo: **Mark Millar**

When we got out there, I was shocked at how big it was compared to what it looked like from land. It really was about 30 foot on the face if not bigger and the waves were really hollow and tubing all the way through to the inside of the reef. The wave faces were smooth and well groomed by the offshore wind. We had lucked into an amazing swell that was for sure! If you haven't been to Mullaghmore then you maybe can't envisage the scene. From out there you can see huge mountains swooping down to the rugged edge of the ocean where long fingers of rock protrude out into a dark ocean. It is a frightening place to be without even considering riding the waves out there. The waves break on a submerged rock ledge that boils and ledges out of every wave as they break onto it. The reef is a large slab of rock with caves and tunnels through it. The waves surge over it and explode on it making the holes in the reef bubble up like a cauldron or a deep sea monster reaching up to pull you under.

I tried to establish some mark ups for Carl to use to drive me in with. We worked out our game plan if something went wrong and after about 30 minutes I jumped into the water and grabbed the rope. I was scared not only because of the surf but because this was the first time I had tow surfed with someone in waves this big. That, unnerved me. I was used to paddling on my own with only me to think of. I was feeling edgy. I remember being more scared than normal in big waves. Yes I had been doing a lot of practicing with Carl in the surf with the ski but I didn't feel confident this day as this was our first proper sized swell together. This was the real deal and I felt uncertain. I suppose it was because I am used to being completely self reliant out there, just me and my board and only me to have faith in. Even when G and Bob were with me I spent more time stressing about them than focusing on catching waves. I'm sure all surfers can relate to being on their own in the surf and for me to now be in a team situation was a bit alien to me even though I had been doing stuff with Carl in smaller surf for some time. I suppose this was the first day I really felt like we were in surf together that was threatening. Only now that the surf was big and angry did I start to feel concerned. We agreed that if we got one wave, we would call it quits for the day and would class the session as successful.

Carl pulled me up and started driving towards the peak. I was fully crapping my pants! I was worried that he would put me somewhere I didn't want to be and I'm sure he was worried that I would get hit and fall. It was a very nervous moment. We missed several waves to begin with which didn't make things any better. It felt awkward and uncomfortable to be honest. We just couldn't connect with the spot. It was probably to do with fear holding us back. I've been in that position in the surf before and I hate the consequences of not being able to overcome the fear. We were considering calling it a day and going in but I know I wouldn't have been content with that plan! I had been there before too many times! Before we knew it, as if Mother Nature was giving us a chance if we wanted it, a wave was coming! It looked like we were going to time it properly and get me onto it. Carl drove towards it at an angle giving me the room to lean out on the rope and go into the wave. I dropped the rope and glided into the wave with the weight of my board helping me to glide into position. Carl drove up onto the shoulder of the wave to get a look at me from above. As I went down it, I knew this was the biggest tow in wave I had ridden yet. I played it safe and angled my board for the channel. I was rigid on the wave, not flexible and free, I was obviously so scared I didn't want to move in case I fell. I was going mach 10! I remember hearing this roar and explosion right beside me and then seeing the huge plume of white water just like I had seen at Mavericks on my first big wave there. I looked over my shoulder to the right and there was a huge barrel churning about arms length from me. I didn't realise I was that deep on the wave! I thought I had played it safer than that! I didn't want to fall so I very gradually turned my head back round so as not to move my body to make me fall. When I looked straight ahead again, I could see Carl on the ski in the corner of my eye and I heard him hooting as the wave broke behind me. He was perched on the top of the shoulder about 25 feet above me. He was obviously stoked! I rode the wave out to the channel and we were high fiving and laughing! It was a good feeling! We persevered and it paid off! We both felt good even though I was the only one riding the wave. He said it made him feel good too because he made it happen.

We did what we wanted to do and that was to ride one and then call it quits. We could have stayed out and got some more but that would have been asking for it! I was scared; any wrong move could have been a disaster. I honestly think we got away with that one and that was enough! Looking back on that session is scary because the equipment was not good. I don't think it was the safest thing to do to be honest now I can look back at it years later knowing full well what the consequences of making mistakes out there can be!

CHAPTER 9

commit

I WENT ON THE trip to Madeira with Cotty and Ralph. We didn't score any really good surf to be honest. We did get a few pretty big days but not the perfection you see in photos from there. The most positive thing that came out of the trip was that Cotty and I realised a real connection between us and we had a similar outlook and desire to ride big waves. I showed him photos of Carl and I that Mark Miller had taken and he was keen to come over and have a go at some of the spots.

Shortly after we got back from Madeira there was a big swell on the weather charts for the west coast. Carl didn't want to go this time so this left me without a partner. This was the thing about tow surfing that was really frustrating for me at the start. I needed a partner who had the same desire to go and surf every time it got big. I also needed a partner who had a similar level of experience and ability as me. That was really bothering me as like any surfer will tell you, it is normal to be doing everything on your own and not having to worry about having someone with you to enable you to do it.

As promised, I phoned Cotty and told him about the swell. He booked a flight right away and planned to fly in the next day right before the swell. He flew in from Bristol at the drop of a hat. There was no way Cotty was going to be able to tow me in but he wanted to come and see the surf anyway and paddle into some big ones with me.

I set off the next day to get Cotty from the airport and we went and paddled a few spots and also Mullaghmore. The swell wasn't as big or as good as the time Carl and I had it but we both got loads of waves and

Right: Cotty after a left hook from Mullaghmore during a big paddle in session in perfect glassy conditions.
Photo: Kelly Allen

because the ski wasn't involved it was so much less stressful! However I knew that the ski was a necessity for when the surf gets super sized and it was just a matter of time until that day came.

What Carl and I did to this point was vital to me and gave me some real experience but I knew that going forward with the right partner was more important.

I decided to ask Cotty if he wanted to try and tow with me. The next time he was over we took the ski out and I began to show him the ropes. All the stuff Carl and I had learned I was able to show him. The thing was, he picked it up in no time. Probably because Carl and I were self taught but then I just had to teach Cotty it. Within a couple of days he had the hang of it. He came back and forth from England and we spent time working together on it. It felt natural, it flowed and worked. It didn't seem like a struggle or unbalanced, it seemed right. We had a similar background, experience and ability and we both had structured our lives to be able to surf as much as possible when conditions were right.

I felt I had to commit to someone and then give it a go. Just as I wanted to feel safe and secure in the team and know that on any given day that I would have a solid tow partner to surf with, the other member of the team needed that too so I needed to commit to one person whoever it may be.

I had to choose to fully commit to someone and that person was Cotty. I chose to commit everything to him. I wanted him to feel that if there was a big swell forecast, bigger than paddleable then he had a tow partner for definite. I believe it is this loyalty and bond that has shaped us as a team above and beyond any other factor. Knowing that each other is there is vital in this and it produced confidence in each other. The weird thing was we were now a tow team but we lived in different countries! You might be wondering how on earth that could have worked but that just high lights even more so, the strength of our bond and team work.

Cotty began coming over every other week or so and we would train and practice in all types and size of waves and various spots so that on the biggest day of the year we would be ready to ride huge waves with confidence.

one step forward...

THE SUN WAS JUST coming up as we reversed the ski down the slip at Mullaghmore harbour on an icy February morning. There were no clouds to keep the heat in despite the sun beginning to rise. A brisk south west wind was blowing in through the mouth of the harbour making putting our wet wetsuits on feel like torture. I am never one for hanging my suit up the night before to let it drip dry. I usually leave it lying in the bucket in the van over night. Every day, I pull it from icy water and curse myself for being so lazy! I once heard it described as like putting on a used condom! Thankfully I have no experience of that!

I fired up the ski as it sat on the slope of the slipway, still on the trailer. Its engine roared round the empty harbour for a few second s before I switched it off. Cotty was standing in the doorway of a closed hotel with his top half fully clothed and his bottom half fully naked! He never travels with a towel but has this knack of tucking his goods up into the bottom of his coat while he slips into his wetsuit.

Once we had our suits and vests on, we backed the ski in. The harbour rippled with the breeze. Despite the cold air and wet wetsuits, we were warm now. We drove out the harbour mouth.

There was no doubt that conditions were good this day. It was straight offshore, the swell was booming in around the point and the sun was shinning. As we drove out we noticed that the surf looked like it was wrapping further round the headland than usual. When we got out to the peak, we realised that it was big, bigger than we had seen it to date out there. It was beautiful. The waves were really blue and the rocky headland didn't look just as menacing as we've seen it before. The sets were a bit inconsistent. We waited and watched for around 20 minutes and only a couple of sets broke. The tide looked to be a little too full meaning that the reef was further under water than would have been ideal. It looked like most of the waves coming through just couldn't feel the bottom and therefore only really peaked up on the reef and didn't really run the full length of it with force. The sets were the only ones that broke properly. Big perfect waves would come along and dwarf everything else that came through. We set up.

I must admit, we were both pretty nervous. It was obvious that if we miss timed it out there we would be in for a good clobbering. When the sets aren't very consistent, it makes it more dangerous as you can get caught out much more easily or become impatient and try and go on a small one.

Cotty towed me first. It was so cold there was a steam rising off the sea. I remember feeling rigid in the cold as I cowardly slipped off the ski into the water desperately trying to keep my head out.

We still only had a crappy water ski rope and no rescue sled. The water ski rope was pink and white and really thin. It is dangerous because the impeller of the ski can take it in and get wrapped in around the shaft. We were always keeping an eye on where the rope was. Carl and I had both run the ski over it a couple of times but I hadn't been able to get one of the specially designed tow surf ones from Hawaii yet. The proper tow surf ones are big thick floating lines that the impeller can't suck into the grill. Therefore they are safer. The only place I know of getting them is from towsurfer.com and they cost almost $200. I still had no sled. They were even harder to get hold off and 5 times more expensive.

Cotty pulled me up. Back then we struggled a little getting to our feet every time so once we were up, we used to do loops with each other on the back of the rope until a good wave came in and then fire each other into it. It was a killer on the arms and thighs, hanging onto the rope for five minutes until a wave came. I think it actually makes you more nervous too. Some sessions we were lucky to get two waves each as we hadn't learned how to consistently time it right and also the fear kept us from fully committing. We were on our own as usual this day. I had called Ritchie the night before to see if he was going to go out too but he had things he needed to take care off and wasn't able to make it. We were well used to being on our own anyway. In fact we had never towed with anyone else. I think we became self reliant and when we only had ourselves out there we depended on just us and that probably made us stronger. Yeah we had crappy equipment for the most part but we made do.

As Cotty drove me round in loops watching the sets approaching, he attempted to put me onto a couple but they didn't really break. It felt like the tide was getting even higher and even the bigger sets coming in from the mouth of Donegal Bay weren't feeling the bottom anymore. He tried to get me on a few and then I was so wrecked from hanging on, I swapped with him. "Cotty, Lets swap, I'll get you onto a few mate!" I shouted. I'm sure he was cold and I was aching so it made sense to switch even though I hadn't ridden a wave yet.

He drove the ski out into the safety of the deep water channel and I climbed up on to it behind him. We both wear 'kill cords' attached to our vests. Only the driver of the ski needs one but if worst came to the worst and we got separated, as long as one person made it to the ski then they could drive it. The engine won't start without a kill cord in place. It's a safety device if anyone falls off, it cuts the engine. We had already experienced that first hand when I went in to pick Cotty up after a wipe out at a spot we call AA's further off the coast. I got him and pulled him on to the back of the ski just before a 20 foot wall of white water was about to hit us. We had no sled so it was harder to do pick ups back then. As I swung him onto the ski that time, the kill cord popped out of its slot and stopped the engine. Cotty was on his knees on the transom of the ski yelling "Go Go Go!!!!" I fumbled with the cord trying to get it into place and at the last minute screamed back "Abort!" Goodness knows why I said 'Abort!' and not "Oh f$%k get the f%$^k off, we're about to get smashed!" Anyway, I chose the polite word abort before we both got hit by the wave, the ski and boards disappeared and we were left swimming after them, three quarters of a mile out to sea. So, we know full well, the importance of a 'Kill Cord'.

I slipped past Cotty on the right of the ski as he slid past me on the left, both trying not to tip the ski and send either of us into the drink. I put my kill cord into the ignition and fired up the engine. Cotty jumped in to the water to get ready. We only had that one board between us and to be honest the straps were a little far apart for Cotty as he is a few inches shorter than me. Cotty goes really purple in the cold so he was more than glad to get into the water as it was warmer than standing on the ski in the wind.

I had spent a bit more time on the ski than Cotty at this stage and felt comfortable driving it. That combined with a solid pulse of swell helped me get him onto three waves in a matter of minutes. It was strange because Cotty struggled for about half an hour to get me on one as the ocean just didn't really send him anything juicy to put me on.

"Right Al, swap, I wanna get you onto one mate!" He was frothing, he'd just had a couple of good ones and then a huge one that looked like it was going to go nuts but after the first peak, it dissipated off as the water was too deep. He climbed onto the ski, he wanted me to get a couple too. That's the thing about tow surfing, it's not as solitary or as selfish as ordinary surfing. I can honestly say and I know Cotty agrees with me on this that I get as much pleasure from putting Cotty onto a bomb and seeing him stoked as I do when I get to ride one. I'm not sure if every team in the world feels the same way but for Cotty and I we both genuinely feel as stoked driving each other as we do riding a wave.

"You Ready, there's a set coming?" he shouts as he puts the kill cord into the ignition. "Yeah let's do it!" I shout back over the sound of the engine. He pulled me up and I could now see the set coming towards us. He circled a couple of times to let the set approach before driving into position. This was in no doubt, the biggest set yet this day. He drove deep behind the peak, fully committing to putting me onto one.

I remember looking ashore at our mark up on land and thinking "I'm gonna be deep on this one!" By deep I don't mean, in deeper water, I mean further into the curl of the wave.

If you can imagine a peaky wave, 30 foot high forming on a reef for a moment, I will try and explain what I mean by deep. The waves at Mullaghmore break to the left as we, the surfers, are looking ashore. So if you were standing watching us surfing from land the waves would be peeling off to your right. To us though, we call this a left hander and therefore it peels in a northerly direction, on this reef in particular, as opposed to a southerly direction. Does that make sense? So, we have worked out by spending time out there, that when a wave approaches the submerged rock ledge, that it breaks more or less in the same spot every time before peeling left along the reef. We have this point marked on land using a lamp post lined up with a wall. So, therefore if I was driving the ski with Cotty on the rope, I want to place him in line with that marker on land as I know that the wave I'm trying to put him on will break right in line with it. If I put him too far to the south of the mark up point the wave will break in front of him and he will either get caught behind a big section of white water or have to pull into the barrel to try and make the ride. If I put him too far to the north of the peak then he will miss the best part of the wave. So, ideally I want to place him right on the middle of the peak where the wave is lined up with the marker on land and where it is first going to break on the reef before peeling north along the reef. Clear as mud you say! Anyway, read on, the best bit is coming up!

So, there is a big one coming, Cotty glances back at me as if to say "You want it?" I nodded in response as I was closely watching the wave line up and stack on the reef. There was no doubt about it, we were deep and it was a big one. I tried to lean out to the right off the wake from the ski to allow myself to swing off the rope before letting go. Cotty ended up driving the ski on to the peak of the wave. The peak is right where I needed to be. I was too far back and I had no way of getting into the wave. The rope went slack as Cotty killed the throttle in an attempt to let the ski drift over the back off the wave. It was too late. The peak of the wave that Cotty was on, turned into the lip of the wave and lifted both Cotty and the ski. I dropped the rope and watched as the 30 foot beast swallowed my tow partner and jet ski. The last thing I saw was Cotty sitting on the ski and then disappearing out of view. The rope handle, that I had just let go off got sucked from in front of me like a shark's tail through water. Thanks goodness I wasn't holding on to it.

I watched as the huge back of the wave ploughed over the reef taking them with it. The rest of the set was still coming, in fact the next wave was even bigger. I was now floating on my tow board with my impact vest on as what looked like a 40 footer began to close in on me. At this point I had two things on my mind. I was wondering if Cotty was ok and also I was trying to make it out from the impact zone as fast as I could as the next wave was starting to bend on the reef and trap me. Paddling a tow board is a headache; the straps get in the way and the vest too. Combined with the fact that it barely floats, it is quite a challenge to move it when you need too! We don't wear leashes on our tow boards as the waves are so big they will break anyway and as the boards are so heavy, the last thing we want is a 10kg weight swinging around attached to us!

As I scrambled to get out of the way of the next one, the bow of the ski surfaced not far from me. The ski kind of rocked backwards and forwards as the wave let it up for air. Just behind it Cotty surfaced. I was glad to see him swimming and in one piece. I made it out of the way of the next one but Cotty and the ski didn't. As I paddled up over it I got a bird's eye view as the wave stood up on the reef, took aim and detonated right in front of Cotty. I kept swimming narrowly avoiding getting completely clobbered by the rest of the set. Every now and again I would get clipped by a big end section of white water that would hiss over me like a fire breathing beast.

That was the last time I saw Cotty until I made it ashore. The swell was so big that I couldn't get out anywhere along the point. Normally it is possible to climb up at the headland but there was a raging rip running and making it difficult to get to that particular spot on the cliff.

I always believe in going with the flow out there. I think it is best to let it take you where it wants and then once things have settled more, work your way back to where you need to be rather than fighting against strong currents.

I still couldn't see Cotty. I knew that the second wave would have blasted him out of danger and into deep water so I had a fair idea he was probably already on land and I just assumed the ski sank.

I eventually climbed out just behind the harbour wall. I was sure Cotty would have been back on land way before me as he had a bit of a helping hand from a wave or two! As I climbed out onto the rocks I realised where he was! Cotty was just off the coast from where I was standing. Like a warrior, he was in the water back stroking towards shore with a leash tied to the front of the ski pulling it as he swam! We always said that if something happened to the ski then one of us would go ashore and get two boards to paddle out to the other one and then both of us would just paddle the ski ashore. As I ran to get the boards I could tell the wind was holding Cotty out there and even though he can swim like an Olympian, he wasn't making any headway and was only holding position. I knew that the two of us would have no problems once I got out there. I pulled out two boards from the van. Just as I closed the doors, the rattle of a helicopter overhead, echoed off the harbour wall. It was the coast guard. It turned out a concerned bystander had seen the whole thing and called for help, unaware that the worst was over and that everything was in hand. The crew winched down and took Cotty off the ski.

I watched as Cotty dangled from the harness and got pulled up into the chopper leaving the ski to its watery grave. Emmet turned up as he had heard the lifeboat had been tasked but didn't launch as the surf was too big to get the boat out. He was worried it was us and after ringing my phone seven times, he jumped in his pick up and drove out. I was standing on the harbour wall as he pulled into the car park. He ran along the quay looking worried. "You ok sham?" he asked. I explained what had happened and he gradually began to relax. I suppose he had thought the worst and as he drove out he probably wasn't sure what to expect upon arrival at the harbour.

I loaded the boards back into the van and began to drive towards Sligo Airbase. The empty trailer rattled behind me as I rushed along the windy road from the harbour to the main Sligo line. News spread quickly about what had happened. My phone started ringing with friends who had heard something had happened and wanted to see if I was ok. Emmet phoned me as he drove to work and said a local radio station had just called him asking for my number but he didn't give it to them. Before long, we were getting calls from lots of unknown numbers and journalists. I made a point of not talking to anyone. It was obvious the whole thing was getting blown out of proportion. I didn't want to tell my Mum but I had to as it was obvious she was going to find out something and it would be best coming from me as at least it would be the truth.

"Mum?" I said. "What's wrong?" she anxiously replied. Isn't it weird that your Mum can always tell when something is wrong even before you tell her! I tried to play it down. I said "Cotty came off the ski, we are both ok, I'm just ringing to tell you as there are lots of journalists looking for a story and I don't want you to hear it on the news first". She was silent for a few seconds then came back with "Where's the ski?" I said "We haven't got it back" I had barely finished speaking and she abruptly said "GOOD!" She wasn't impressed to say the least! She couldn't understand why it might be on the news. I suppose at that time tow surfing was still small time and barely recognised in Ireland and Europe for the most part.

I arrived at the air base and Cotty was sat there in his wetsuit looking really worried. As I walked in the door, his glum face looked up from the table he was sat at. The first words he said were "Mate, I'm sorry, I'm so sorry!" He was obviously expecting me to be gutted about the ski. I hadn't even thought about that. This was the first time I'd seen him since he disappeared over the falls of that wave he tried to tow me into. I was glad to see he was unhurt. He explained that the engine wouldn't start although it didn't have any water in it.

We thanked the guys for their assistance and then left the base. We were annoyed that someone called them out as although it might have looked like we didn't have it under control to an onlooker, we did and if the helicopter hadn't turned up it would have just been a matter of paddling the ski ashore. Although, the flip side of that is that had something gone wrong badly then that bystanders actions had the helicopter with us within minutes and they would have been able to act immediately. We are grateful that the bystander made that decision.

We were getting constantly hassled by journalists, nosey people and doubters on the phone. We all agreed not to say anything to anyone. We didn't want to go back to Bundoran but we had to try and find the ski. We drove along the coast trying to find it but the sea was so big that it was like looking for a needle in a haystack. We decided we should drive south and try and avoid all the people trying to talk to us and let the controversy die down a wee bit. We drove to a little village called Easkey and parked up outside the village on the verge. I then got a phone call from my Mum saying that her Mum had just passed away. I didn't mention this to Cotty, I just said nothing. He was in enough shock without adding that to the mix. I spoke to Mum and she said there was nothing I could do and that I should stay where I was until I got everything sorted out. She had her sisters around her and they were all dealing with funeral arrangements.

We were parked up on a stretch of coast beside a well known surf spot, Easkey Right. The ruin of a castle stood just behind us. The conditions and the surf was a mess. There were no surfers or cars around. Then one car came along the lane, it continued on past us but the guy driving it had a good look in at us. I looked in the rear view mirror as he passed and he put his brakes on and began to reverse back. He pulled up beside my window. I was expecting him to be looking for directions but when I rolled the window down he shouted over "Are you Al Mennie?" I said "Yeah" "I just heard what happened! You guys have balls! Fair play to you! I hope you are all ok" He rolled up his window and drove off. We couldn't believe that we were over an hours drive away from Mullaghmore and already news was spreading like wild fire.

**Battered equipment. Pre
Aileen's Tow in session,
October 2009.**

Photo: Conn Osborne

Right: **Cotty fits a heavy duty
knee brace to support his
ruptured ACL ligament, before
an Aileen's session, 2009.**

Photo: Conn Osborne

Cotty and I leaving
Doolin harbour, Co. Clare,
October, 2009.
Photo: Conn Osborne

Right: This is me paddling
into a wave at Aileen's, Co.
Clare on my 10'0". Notice
the boils in the water in
front of me.
Photo: Conn Osborne

G spot, an offshore reef break off the west coast of Ireland.
Photo: Kelly Allen

Left: This is me riding a wave after Cotty has towed me in during our first session at Aileen's.

Photo: Kelly Allen

Left bottom: This is me at the end of a ride at Mullaghmore Head, Co. Sligo on December 1st, 2007.

Photo: Kelly Allen

Above (both): This is me surfing Mavericks, Half Moon Bay, California, 2003.

Photo: Tony Canadas

101

Left: **This is my 10'8"
shaped by Northern
Ireland based Rosy
Surfboards.**

Photo: Leah Russell

Below: **This shows the pier
at the end of Castlerock
beach engulfed by a big
winter swell.**

Photo: Johnny Vance

Bottom: Cotty, airlift.

Photo: Kelly Allen

Right: Cool Dude!, Me aged 11 at Castlerock.

Photo: Dad

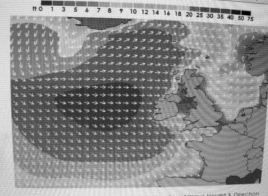

0600 Sat 1st Dec   (24hr)

Significant Wave Height & Direction
Issued at 0600 30th Nov 2007 GMT

Photos from top to bottom...

December 1st 2007, swell chart.
Image www.magicseaweed.com,
Photo: Kelly Allen

Battered ski.
Photo: Kelly Allen

**Duncan and I looking cold at
Doolin harbour January 2007.**
Photo: Aaron Pierce

Top left: The tower over looking Doolin harbour and Crab Island.

Top right: This is me paddling into a wave at Mullaghmore Head December 2008.

Above: This is me narrowly avoiding getting eaten alive by a wild December wave at Mullaghmore. The wind at this spot can make paddling into big waves extremely difficult.

Photos from top to bottom:

I'm outrunning an avalanche after missing a pick up of Cotty during a session in November 2009. Cotty is buried beneath the white water after falling and suffering injuries to his legs.

Photo: Conn Osborne

Cotty and I check out Mullaghmore before paddling out, March 2006.

Photo: Kelly Allen

Aileen's, flawless and in the 70 ft range. Surf was so big the harbour we launch at was swamped by surf leaving us landlocked and frustrated.

Photo: Aaron Pierce

Cotty comes out of the tube on the inside section of Aileens as I follow on the ski to pick him up.

Photo: Aaron Pierce

Top left: Mikee Hamilton looks on as I bottom turn at Mullaghmore. Previous to this wave, I fell and my board disappeared under water for 10 minutes before surfacing with a huge gash in it.

Photo: Aaron Pierce

Middle: Paul O'Kane and I taking a breather moments after I took a serious wipe out at Mullaghmore.

Photo: Aaron Pierce

Top right: This is me at Aileen's on a perfectly symmetrical peak in December 2007. The rest of the waves this day were a fair bit smaller than this and I just got lucky!

Photo: Aaron Pierce

Opposite top: Aussie transplant Paul O'Kane on edge at Mullaghmore.

Photo: Aaron Pierce

Below: Emmet and I paddling out at Aileens after navigating the goat trail and getting pounded in the rocks along the shoreline. I had the flu this day but couldn't sit and watch. Notice how sheer the cliffs are.

Photo: Aaron Pierce

Top: The significance of the session can be gauged on the amount of laughter in the car park afterwards. Mikee, Duncan, Cotty and I buzzing.

Photo: Aaron Pierce

Left: Dawn anticipation, on a bitterly cold January morning 2004.

Photo: Kelly Allen

Below: Dunluce Castle perched on the cliff top above a perfect peaking wave off The Causeway Coast, Northern Ireland.

Photo: Gary McCall

Top left: This is me during a paddle in session at Crab Island, Co. Clare during a windy October swell, 2009.
Photo: Gary McCall

Right: Competitors meeting before the APT World Tow In Cup Championship at Punta do Lobos, Pichelimu, Chile, 2008.
Photo: Tim Ditty

Top right: Surfing Whiterocks Beach, Northern Ireland.
Photo: Gary McCall

Below: In the tube beneath Dunluce Castle, on The Causeway Coast.
Photo: Gary McCall

This is me at Mullaghmore November 2009.
Photo: Aaron Pierce

Cotty speeding down the face of a Mullaghmore wave.
Photo: Aaron Pierce

Notice the rock boils and ledges in the face of the wave and beside my board. Seconds after this photo, the wave detonated on top of me.
Photo: Aaron Pierce

Aussie, Paul O'Kane, and Barry Mottershead watch from the channel as Aileen's throws out a perfect tube onto the reef.
Photo: Aaron Pierce

We later heard a report on the radio about us despite neither of us speaking to any journalists.

We tried to work out on the map where the wind was likely to take the ski. We had a rough idea but we figured there was no point looking until someone reported it. That night was strange as we stayed at Emmet's flat. We were all in shock as to the drama that had come from our surf session. We weren't really in shock from what had happened more because Chinese whispers had started and we were beginning to hear all sorts of crazy fabrications. One of the best was the one about us coming off the ski and the ski washing into the cliff and blowing up into a fire ball.

That night we got to watch the footage that videographer Anthony Butler had recorded. Anthony, or Mr. B as he is more commonly known, had been filming quite a few of our sessions to this point as he wanted to include a big wave section in his DVD 'Performing Monkeys'. This was the first time I had seen what had happened. Cotty had tried to explain it to me but actually getting to watch it back was amazing. We huddled round the TV in Emmet's living room as Anthony set up the camera to play it on the screen. He was keen to get our reaction when we first saw it so he filmed us watching it with another camera.

We watched as Cotty circled the ski round to line up for the peak of the wave. Then we saw the rope go slack just as the wave lurched up to what Emmet measured on the screen to be 30foot high. The wave's lip pushed the ski and Cotty out into the air. Cotty had nowhere to go so dove from the ski. He completely left the ski mid air and penetrated the surface of the wave right in the trough after freefalling from the lip. Thankfully he did penetrate because the ski fell from the lip of the wave and spun 180 degrees through the air before landing right on top of where Cotty had entered the water. The ski didn't penetrate the surface but the wave was so big and hollow that its lip threw out far enough to completely tube over both of them. Neither the ski nor Cotty surfaced for a good few seconds. We could just see me paddling over the next one before it hit Cotty and the ski. Cotty swam so quickly after it, obviously trying to get to it so he would be able to go back out and pick me up. He was clearly wondering if I was getting pummelled by the same waves.

The next morning we were just about to leave when Bundoran man Jimmy Meehan pulled up beside us and said "Lad's your ski is at Rossnowlagh!" We immediately drove to the nearby beach to check it out. We were surprised it even washed up let alone that far away from Mullaghmore. We didn't know what to expect, we didn't stop to ask Jimmy any questions. Rossnowlagh is one of the few beaches that cars are allowed onto so we drove the van on at the south end of the beach and as we anxiously started to head along the strand, we could see what looked to be our ski up near the rocks in front of the caravan park. As we got closer we realised it wasn't our entire ski! It had been ripped apart! I stepped out of the van in disbelief. The red seats were gone altogether and the engine compartment was filled to the brim with densely packed sand. The centre seating console was smashed and strands of glass fibre were hanging out of it. The steering console was also gone, ripped from the ski altogether leaving the twisted handle bars dangling off the side. The bow hatch was also completely gone, ripped out at the hinges. It was a ruin of a ski. Cotty and I were in shock for a few minutes. We didn't know what to do. It was obvious it was never going to be at sea again!

I went off to a nearby building site to find a forklift. There was no way we could get it onto the trailer in that state. The winch wouldn't hold it. I came across a few guys who were putting up a holiday home about a mile away. They were standing on the roof lifting tiles off a big yellow 4 x 4 fork lift. As I walked across the site I was trying to decide what I was going to say to them. I mean, how could I explain this one to a stranger? They followed me down to the beach and they looked as shocked as we were at first. They put the forks under the ski and lifted it up to the car park. We positioned the trailer under it hoping it wouldn't give way with all the extra weight from the sand and the driver set it onto it for us. A few people began to gather to see what was going on. I gave the guys a few Euros for their help and then we left for the airport. If you remember how embarrassed I was driving around with my big new flashy jet ski on the back well now imagine how I felt as I drove into Belfast to leave Cotty and Anthony to the airport with the carcass of the same jet ski dragging behind me! We were getting so many weird looks!

The next few weeks were crazy. So many stories were flying around. There is a saying in Portrush that 'If you fart on Ramore Head, you've s$%t yourself by the time you get to Hillcrest'. Ramore Head is a local headland and Hill Crest is the top of the hill about a mile away. Numerous internet sites ran their own version of events and all the doubters sat at their desks bitching and running us down behind aliases on internet chat rooms. I began to realise who my friends were. It was obvious to me at this moment in time who my true friends were and even more obvious who wasn't. It reminded me a bit of the time the body boarder told me I was going to come back in a box from Mavericks. It was like everyone who doubted us or thought we were reckless or stupid was having their field day. The whole thing affected me in a personal way. I took it very personally and I began to retreat into myself in many ways. I didn't speak to people that much after it happened. By that I mean, I would have gone to the beach to surf and pretty much kept to myself. I would have avoided conversations with people as much as possible. I had no way of explaining to people what happened as there was no way they wanted to believe or understand it even if they heard it first hand from me. I chose to say nothing. My story wasn't as good as the rumours that were floating around anyway and as people always seem to choose the worst case scenario as the true story there was no point in me telling the facts. As I said, I kept myself to myself. I was annoyed that some of the people I would have called friends chose to make up their own stories instead of even asking if we were ok.

People were calling us irresponsible for going out there on our own. The thing they forget is that most of the time we have no choice. There isn't an abundance of big wave surfers here. There aren't even that many people that think big wave surfing is possible in Ireland. It was as if people expected that if we were going to ride waves of that size that we would have back up skis and safety boats waiting to pluck us from danger if anything went wrong. That is the case in Hawaii where big wave surfing is well accepted and lots of people are doing it. This isn't Hawaii, surfing was only beginning to become recognised as possible in Ireland by the general public. We didn't have access to lots of people who were trained in high surf rescue or had skis or boats. The one team we knew that might have been available to go out with us couldn't make it. In fact we had never tow surfed with another team at that point, ever. We were always on our own. Are we seriously expected to not follow our dreams and passions because there was no one else available with the same ambitions? The only way boundaries get pushed is by someone doing it and we weren't about to sit and wait until someone was willing to go with us. It never crossed our minds to not go out if we had no back up. We didn't have any option for back up so it was either do nothing or go at it alone as usual. Ideally we would have had another tow team or at least someone capable in surf rescue on another ski, or a safety boat. We didn't have funding for any of that. We were completely self-funded. We knew by not having back up we were increasing the risk involved but we accepted the risks long before this happened. We both knew and accepted that if you go into the Ocean on days like that then you have to expect to get your ass kicked and pay your dues. Both of us had been riding big waves for some time and although we had ridden consistently bigger waves all our lives, we had also taken consistently worse beatings in the process. It's funny how sometimes when people see us riding huge waves in a picture or a video clip they are blown away by the size of it and they praise us etc. As soon as we take a wipe out people call us irresponsible. I suppose it is down to a lack of understanding of what we are doing.

THE LYRICS OF AMERICAN band 'Hatebreed' have taught me a few lessons over the years. One of my favourite lyrics is 'Never let go of what you strive for, hold tight, never let go!" This never seemed so fitting to the current situation. We were both down, we had taken a physical hit by Mrs. Mullaghmore and a psychological hit as a result of it. The referee was counting to ten. There was no doubt that we were going to get back up. The very next day after losing the ski we paddled Mullaghmore, almost as big as the previous day.

Cotty got checked out by the doctor and was given the all clear. We were without a ski though. I think our biggest fear was that we didn't want a massive swell to show up and have no way of riding it.

We were lucky in that the winter swells stopped right after that big one and we had time to get ourselves and our equipment together.

Someone donated a sled to us, we got some new tow boards made and got a new rope. We were ready for the next big swell.

Although we had all our equipment sorted and we were training a lot with the sled practicing pick ups and rescue scenarios in the surf we were both definitely a little hindered by our thoughts.

I remember being on waves after Cotty towing me in and worrying about Cotty rather than focusing on riding the waves. I would be worrying about where he was and was he ok. I suppose it's a normal thing to go through. We were a team and I think going through the jet ski wipe out was either going to make us stronger or destroy us. It was really difficult for a while. He was obviously struggling too and we weren't as confident or as tight. I do believe it was our true desire to ride big waves that pulled us through it. We really wanted to ride big waves and nothing was going to stop us.

Dave Blount and John McCarthy had been riding bigger and bigger waves at 'Aileens' also towing with one ski. Dave had made a call that a 4.4m swell at 14 seconds coming out of a hurricane just offshore was going to make Aileens break big on September 30th 2006. It was just the day before and Cotty jumped on a flight.

This would be the first time we would surf down there and from what we had heard, this swell was going to be the biggest Aileens had been ridden yet.

We drove 5hr 30mins south through the night in torrential rain. I always remember the date of this swell as my friend Mark rang me in the middle of the night to tell me that his girlfriend, Norma had just given birth to their baby boy Joel.

We arrived at Doolin harbour at 4.30am and climbed into the back of the van to try and sleep for a couple of hours. Of course we were both so anxious and excited that we just lay and talked about what it might be like. I had surfed around this area lots of times in the past but not yet at Aileens. Just off the coast of Doolin harbour is a small island, called Crab Island. It is only about 200meters across and rises out of the water maybe 30 feet at the highest point. It is covered in big slabs of rock.

Left: This is me securing the rescue sled to the ski, the tighter the better!
Photo: Conn Osborne

On top of it is a little round building which I believe was where a monk used to live. A good surf spot breaks off the island. It has always been regarded as a bit of a crazy spot and only suited to experienced surfers. This is still true today, although the level of craziness in terms of the size and types of waves being surfed in Ireland was rapidly rising. Waves like Crab or pmpa in Bundoran were beginning to seem less intimidating than previously due to bigger and more dangerous waves being found and ridden.

Behind Crab Island is a tall round tower which is sited near the top of the cliff, maybe a couple of miles away, looking over the area. Dark thick clouds loomed just above it.

On this day a few tow teams from England came over to surf the same swell at Aileens. These guys had been tow surfing a spot off Newquay called 'The Cribber'. It was famous as it just happened to be right in the heart of Britain's surf capital so if the waves ever got big enough for it to break then it would make headline news in local press. In fact the day we lost the ski, photos appeared in a national paper of the guys riding the Cribber. The photos showed them surfing some big waves. There was no doubt about that. They too didn't have all the equipment, some of them didn't have life vests, sleds or even tow boards. The one difference I really noticed was that the waves they were riding, although they were big, didn't appear to have the shape and the volume that we were used to seeing here.

I knew all the guys from doing contests or surf trips before. Cotty and I got out of the van from two hours of not sleeping for a bit of a catch up. Duncan Scott, Russell Winter, Spencer Hargreaves, Dan Joel, Sam Lamiroy and Ian Battrick had all driven through the night to get here just like us. They had managed to secure a sponsorship deal with an energy drink brand and also from wetsuit company O'Neill to fund their trip and then tied it all in with Carve surf Magazine. This was frustrating for us as we had been trying to secure some sort of backing too but we found that we spent more time riding big waves as they were so readily available and not enough time on the business end of things as it is riding the big waves that we were most interested in. These guys didn't have the big waves consistently on their shores so they appeared to have spent that time chasing good funding deals so they could go where the big waves were.

It was only getting bright and the rain was still falling really hard. We all compared equipment and checked out each others skis as we set everything up. I noticed how some of their tow boards were actually just like ordinary short boards with straps on them rather than heavy like ours. It looked like they were shaped by good shapers but they didn't appear to be specifically for the kind of waves we get here. They were obviously still trying to feel their way through the thing too. Duncan Scott was the best prepared. Duncan had a good board, well weighted, and had already some experience from surfing big waves. Duncan is a Manchester born, South African, Newquay surfer. I am actually lost as to his true nationality and age yet I've known him for years. He has surfed Dungeons in South Africa, spent time in Hawaii and competed professionally, the list goes on. On this day he teamed up with Dave Blount as John McCarthy was out of the country.

Cotty and I were not used to having other teams with us; we did this always on our own. These guys had towed a lot less than us but they had done so among other teams. Cotty and I were excited to be with other guys and also a little weary of it as we were thinking there might be a bit of a traffic jam out there.

We all put our skis in except Russ and Spenny. These guys need no introduction, they are without doubt two of the most successful surfers to ever come out of Britain. They decided they wanted to go and check out the break from the cliff top before they launched. Aileens breaks at the foot of the cliffs of Moher. The cliffs are over 700 feet high and it is almost impossible to get to the bottom of them except for a small goat trail which happens to be right in front of the surf spot. On this day though, it was going to be impassable as the rain was washing it away. They went for a look from the cliff top as we all began to head out on the skis. A local skipper was hired along with his rib to take a few people out

to take photos including Englishman Mickey Smith. The rib headed off in front of the skis. In fact everyone followed it but Cotty and I. We were lagging behind a little as we loaded our kit onto the ski in the harbour.

To get out there to Aileens we had to drive the ski through the huge surf at Crab Island. As I said, I have surfed Crab loads of times but I had never seen waves this big breaking across the deep water channel. We had to drive quickly and avoid getting picked off by the shifting waves. Once we cleared the break zone around the island we were out in deep water heading south towards the big dark evil looking cliffs. The swell lines were coming at us from the west and as we drove up over the top of one swell line we could see that the whole way to the horizon was lined up like corduroy. Then we would drive down into the trough of the next hoping that the one over the next wasn't going to cap and catch us out. We had lost sight of the other skis and boat although we had a fair idea were we needed to be headed so we kept motoring on out. We were driving for about ten minutes when we started to get in front of the cliffs. I don't know if you have ever seen photos or postcards of the cliffs but I can tell you, they are very imposing. It was a really cloudy day, the wind was blowing and it was raining constantly. A mist had formed at the top of the cliffs making them appear to have no top. There was a real dark, evil feel to the location. I've heard people describe it as like a scene from Lord of the Rings. I have never seen that film so I don't know but I hear people say that all the time. We couldn't get a scale on things as we had never been there before. The cliffs stretch for a few miles to the south. All we could see were these huge black cliffs with white water breaking the whole way along the bottom of them. In the distance we could see a white water peak breaking further out to sea than the rest of the waves. "That must be it there mate!" proclaimed Cotty. We kept heading in that direction. I was holding on really tight as the surface was bumpy and he was driving fast as we wanted to get there quickly. We

Left: Cotty and I heading down the goat trail at Aileen's. The boulders at the bottom are bigger than a family car and make the paddle out tricky especially when it's really big out there.
Photo: Kelly Allen

were both nervous as this was our first proper big swell since losing the ski. Obviously we were thinking about that a lot. I was looking to my left just trying to take in the location as we drove. I was wondering how on earth we were going to deal with something going wrong. There was no way anyone would be able to get out of the rocks at the bottom of the sheer cliffs in swell this size. As I scanned along the cliffs, still clinging on for dear life, something caught my eye at the bottom. It was the rib. I could just make out the purple tubes on it in between the passing waves. "It's in there Cotty!" I screamed over the engine. He let go of the throttle and responded with "Oh my Lord!" We sat on the ski for a few minutes looking at the rib. All of a sudden the cliffs looked twice as big as now we had some scale on the place. The boat looked tiny. We couldn't even see the skis at this stage. The white water looked so big and the waves looked to be all over the place and out of control. We were about a mile out at this stage. We started driving in towards the boat.

The scene was frightening and overwhelming. I was in shock as to what was actually going on. The cliffs were f"£kin huge. They towered over us like the grim reaper waiting to feast on an unsuspecting surfer. We pulled up in the deep water channel just in time to see a thick, stormy wave maul through the line up. It looked out of control. The other skis and teams were just sitting watching it from the channel. No one seemed interested in having a go. There was real feel of shock in the air. Not so much because of the waves themselves but the whole scene. The waves were breaking a couple of hundred yards clear of the cliff base onto a boiling, ledging reef. Cotty and I always look for the worst case scenario before we even consider riding a wave. It was obvious that if you fell out there you were going to get severely beaten and washed over the reef and into a bay. The bay was completely back dropped by the cliffs with no way up or down. The only way back out was to wait until your tow partner would come in and get you. We could see huge black boulders, the size of cars and houses littering the shore line. Getting someone from in there with the ski was going to require skill and taking a lot of risk. We know that our ski is our lifeline but we are always prepared to have to swim too. We were swimmers and surfers before we had a jet ski however it looked virtually impossible to be able to swim through the shore line and deal with the huge white water. We checked it all out as best we could and agreed that if one of us went down and got washed in there that they would wait it out until the other was able to get the ski in safely and pick them up. If one of us got hurt and couldn't swim to the ski then we agreed that the other would have to try and beach the ski as best he could so that it would at least survive getting pounded in the rocks until both of us could get back on it.

There was no doubt about it that the scenarios and eventualities which may arise were unique. The wave itself hadn't really become an issue to us. We weren't really intimidated by it, more so what could happen after a fall. This wasn't like Mullaghmore in that after you fall, you get rolled over the reef for a bit and then as the wave runs off the back of the reef into deep water everything is ok. The scenarios that could arise out at Aileens appeared that they would get worse after a fall. The wipe out would only be the beginning of the nightmare.

We were content with our 'disaster plans' and began to set up. Russ and Spenny arrived and looked in shock. Cotty slipped into the water and got into his straps. "I won't kill you!" I shouted. He laughed back at me. I pulled him up and headed out past the other teams to try and get a few. I was nervous. I was worried about what could happen. The other teams were sat in the channel obviously waiting to see if we would get one.

I saw an average one coming through and I shouted "You ready?" "Yeah mate, let's do it!" Cotty responded. The butterflies in my tummy were making me uneasy and even more nervous. I drove Cotty into the approaching wave from the deep water channel so that I could place him on the wave but only on the shoulder. I didn't want to put him right on the peak on the first one. By putting him on the shoulder it allowed him to fade to whatever position he wanted without feeling like I'd trapped him too deep. He dropped the rope and faded into the wave. As he disappeared into the trough I noticed how raw and angry the wave looked. It was streaked with froth and the wind whipped the top off it. Obviously the hurricane was not far away and the swell was generated so close to shore that it hadn't settled down and was just raging through. I followed along on the ski hoping he wasn't going to fall. Even the slightest bit of chop can cause problems at high speed and the waves were really bumpy this day. On top of that our nerves were making us rigid and not relaxed. As I drove behind the wave I kept glancing at the other skis and boat to see the reactions of the other guys. They were positioned further in towards the cliff and could therefore watch Cotty surf the wave from a better vantage point. I knew that if he fell they would react and then I would know to start looking for him. He kicked out the back of the wave on the inside and I went in to pick him up. As I spun the ski around to allow him to climb onto the sled, I looked back over my left shoulder. As I watched him grab the handle I saw a huge black shelf of rock surge out of the water as the waves drained off it, just feet behind him. When I looked forward again to pull the throttle the next wave had bent round in front of us trapping us between it and the dry ledge. I had nowhere to run except with the wave. I gunned the ski towards the 20 foot wall of dark green water and tried to out run it along its face. It was getting steeper and steeper and we were going flat out. Beneath us the black uneven edge of the rock ledge was waiting for us and above us the lip was beginning to feather. I managed to sneak us up over the back of it just before it broke on the reef. That was a close call, and that was only the first wave ridden that day!

Cottys next one was a screamer. He faded across into the peak of the wave and then dropped down it as a huge barrel broke behind him. He navigated his way round a mountainous section of avalanching white water and into the channel.

The other guys were now set up and also trying to get some waves. The stand out was no doubt Duncan Scott. He looked much more comfortable than anyone else. Russ and Spenny were surfing with ease and fluidity like the waves were two foot! Both of them carving lines across the beasts as most of us ran for cover. In fact, Spenny fell at one stage and got washed through into the rocks. Russ couldn't find him for ages and was jumping over white water waves and through rocks on the ski trying to find him. The rocks protruding through the white surface were making it difficult to spot him. He got him just in time and then made it back out without any problems. It was like he had to run into a lions den to pick up a bit of meat and get out again with out getting eaten.

Cotty switched with me and began to put me onto a few. I was really worried at this stage. I was worried because I was scared for Cotty. It was such a psychological battle out there anyway but even more so for Cotty. He must have been thinking about losing the ski at Mullaghmore. Nevertheless, he manned up a lot more than I did. I was scared. He was putting me onto waves that were huge and I should have gone but I pulled back because I was scared. I didn't go on some of them. The ones I went on I only rode out on the shoulder so I wouldn't get clipped. Later in the session I became a bit more comfortable and confident and I actually rode a few bombs by the end of it.

**This is me during my
first surf at Aileens.**
Photo: Kelly Allen

Everyone was getting huge waves and no one had been hurt. As the tide dropped the waves got a little more organised. We surfed for six hours that day. It was so eventful that it only seemed like two hours! Everyone was high fiving at the harbour when we got back. There was a real buzz and energy amongst us. Everyone was talking about it and recalling their waves. A few of us were watching as Duncan was in full display and animation while describing one of his rides. I could see the passion in his eyes. It was a great feeling being part of that session. We were so used to being alone and it was reassuring having more than just us to rely on. Looking back on it, that swell probably would have gone unridden had Cotty and I turned up on our own. Having others around was a confidence boost in some ways.

CHAPTER 12

no access

OUR ALARM WENT OFF at 630am. I sheepishly rolled out of my bunk into the openness of the icy dormitory and hurried on my clothes. It was pitch black outside and the heating in the hostel we had slept in hadn't been on all night. I was shivering with cold. You know that cold that penetrates right through to your bones. I was exhausted from the drive down. We travelled through the night and it took us 8 hours as the roads were so icy. From time to time the trailer would appear in the wing mirror as it slid sideways round corners behind the van! We actually had to stop once to help someone who had crashed. We had stayed in a little hostel in Doolin. It was a cold February morning in 2007. We went into the kitchen which was like a school canteen with big stainless steel units along the walls. It was barely bright outside so we put the kettle on to make tea to try and warm us up before going outside to scrape ice off the ski and van windows.

We pulled into the harbour to get our first look at the swell. The swell was forecast to be 6.6metres which for Aileen's was going to be huge. We were the only ones in the harbour. The crew that came over from England for a previous big session had obviously had their fill of it and we were back to being on our own. We could see this swell was perfect, it was off the Richter! I timed the waves with my watch and worked out that the wave period was 21 seconds meaning that the waves were spaced 21 seconds apart from each other resulting in a really well organised, clean swell. Waves were exploding all over the place; huge walls of water were peeling their way ashore from what looked like miles out to sea. The slip way at which we normally launch was swamped with head high waves breaking on it and over it and washing all the way up into the car park. We stood there alone looking at the slip way trying to figure out how we could get the ski in and more importantly how we would get it back out. We considered tying it to a rope and lowering it in from the back of the van so we wouldn't get the van swamped but the surf was too strong to let us away with that idea. We considered dumping the ski off the trailer at the top of the slip and letting the back wash float it and then suck it out with it. We were getting some crazy ideas! Our gateway to the surf was closed! It was so frustrating, we were faced with the biggest, cleanest surf we had ever seen and we knew Aileen's would be about twice the size of a house! This is what we dream of, riding waves of epic proportions and they were right in front of us. The only thing was we couldn't get out there. I don't know if you can comprehend the frustration we were experiencing. I suppose it is like when climbers go to the base of a mountain after planning everything to the finest detail only to be held back by some adverse condition or occurrence they had never foreseen. Everything we train for and plan for had arrived yet we hadn't ever considered or planned for the slip way to be impassable despite it happening at other spots in the past... We had been towing and paddling a spot off the west coast of Donegal and when we came in to bring the ski out of the water, the swell was completely swamping the slip. We couldn't get the ski out and ended up driving back out to sea at almost dark and driving through 6metre swells for 30 minutes to the next harbour. This got us thinking. We knew of another more sheltered harbour to the south end of the cliffs at Liscannor. I was sure we would get it in there. I spoke to a local guy for his input and he explained that he had driven a ski around that southern end of the cliffs on a much smaller day and experienced crazy water movement out there. He said that the water is so deep that the huge swells hit the cliff without breaking first causing massive backwash.

He was sure it would be really dangerous to even attempt this in seas so big. We knew that if something went wrong at Aileen's and we needed to beach the ski we would have to drive south to Lahinch anyway. We drove up to the cliffs to get a look at the swell from above. Huge clean, lines of swell were stacked and marching in from the horizon. The Ocean looked corrugated as far as the eye could see. We studied the entire break zone for about 45 minutes. It was obvious that if one of us fell we were going to be in for a long night on the rocks. The rescue area and safety channel was completely closing out. One mistake and the surfer was going to be on his own until the swell backed off enough to let the driver in to get him. We actually have survival packs in our ski. The kit is full of all the normal marine safety kit but also we keep food rations, survival bags, thermal wear, torches, an axe and a tent. It is shrink wrapped to keep it in good condition. This is all great as long as no one gets hurt and needs immediate medical attention. The base of the cliffs is virtually inaccessible from sea in these conditions, the cliff is too unstable to winch down and a helicopter would need a line about 700feet long! At this point we were beginning to realise that it was going to be a suicide mission if we were to attempt this on our own. Sometimes one or two mistakes are manageable but this swell was not going to allow us that luxury. One mistake on this day and the consequences could be terminal!

As we walked back up the hill to the van we were seriously confused. I had feelings of frustration and shock. "For F$%k Sake! This is the day of all f$%kin days and we are standing right in front of it and we can't f$%kin get out there!" I was angry too. I couldn't believe that we had no way of accessing it. I wasn't sure about the local guy saying it was impassable from the south. I was sure I could make it. As we drove over the top of the hill just before the visitors centre at the cliffs we could see Liscannor Bay. Liscannor bay is deep narrow bay that runs in from Spanish point at the western tip into the small town of Lahinch. Usually if Aileen's is in the 40 foot range we would see a few waves breaking out in the bay on shallow banks of sand or rock. On this day we could see that waves were breaking the whole way across the bay. It was obvious that the access to the south of the cliffs was being blocked by waves which must have been at least 40 feet. When we pulled into the small harbour there was even more chaos. The harbour appeared full of water, almost bursting over the wall. The wall wraps right around the harbour and there is a narrow mouth out into the bay. The mouth of the harbour had 12 foot waves washing past it. As the waves washed past the mouth of the harbour they surged into it making the water wash round the perimeter of it. Then the water would suck out again taking every last drop with it and leaving the harbour completely drained exposing its muddy, sandy bottom before the next surge came in. As this happened, the concrete slip way was left hanging in mid air with a six foot drop before the water would fill back in again. Not much of a harbour eh? Imagine running from a storm at sea in your boat to the nearest harbour to find not even enough water to safely float your boat!

We had finally agreed that we were going to have to abandon surfing the biggest waves of our lives at Aileen's on this swell. It was not sensible. Maybe you don't think any of this is sensible but to us this time there were too many variables weighted against us and not enough in our favour. As much as we wanted to ride what looked like 70 foot waves, we knew that we would literally be toying with death. Maybe you think we do that all the time anyway, and this was no different. Usually we have a plan so if something goes wrong we have a way of getting control of everything again. This swell was leaving us no options other than to ride the big waves and not fall. Both Cotty and I know that is not realistic and it is normal for wipe outs to occur no matter how optimistic we might be. There was no way of rescuing each other if something went wrong which could result in serious consequences. We decided to let this one go.

However...As some of the other local surfers headed to a more sheltered location further north were the waves were supposed to be smaller and fun, Cotty and I backed the ski down the slip. We weren't about to let this swell go without nailing a few rides. We knew Aileen's was off the cards but we could see that on the other side of the bay, about 2 miles away, huge waves were peeling for some time before closing out across the bay. We were keen to give it a go. The ski sat on the slip waiting for the surge. We had literally seconds to put the ski in as soon as the harbour level raised enough to just cover the end of the concrete. We had it all untied and just sitting on the trailer, still hitched onto the van. Cotty was standing with it as I sat in the van waiting for his call. "Go mate!" He shouted. I stuck the van in reverse and backed down the slip quickly before slamming the brakes on. The ski then fired off the back and into the swirling harbour. As I pulled the van away, Cotty launched himself into the harbour after the ski, inserted his kill cord and started the engine. He had to go with the flow of water out the harbour mouth as it drained into the surf. Then as it filled back up again he came in really fast, picked me up along with our boards and we raced back out before it dried out again! Craziness!

As soon as we cleared the harbour wall we were side on to huge walls of white water. Cotty had to drive really quickly to sneak through, over and round lots of waves before we got out far enough to only have to dodge the really big ones. We were driving at about 35 knots constantly. The surface was choppy and turbulent and I struggled to hang on to both the boards and Cotty. It was like a mine field out there. Huge bombs were detonating all around us. Cotty kept trying to point the ski in the direction of a hotel on the far side of the bay but every now and again we would look back at it and notice we had gone completely of course as we had to continually out run avalanches. Eventually we got to the other side of the bay, the most southern side. It was a bit more protected and allowing the waves to peel along the edge of its reefs. The session itself was a lot more uneventful than the journey across the bay. The waves were fat, sloppy but still really big. I think we were just disheartened after having to abandon the opportunity to ride giant Aileen's. This session turned into more of a training session than a memorable surf session. We had some crazy pick ups to do which involved out running 20foot walls of white water for about 500 yards at times with the throttle fully open. It was amazing being out there. We both got a few rides and then started to make a run for it back through the mine field. We got trapped with no where to run at one stage and had to take a big wall of white water on the bow. It knocked Cotty off the ski along with our boards. I eventually got them all back on and got us into the harbour. The thing was, the tide had dropped more and the slip was now hanging out of the harbour more than before. Cotty took the ski and burned back out of the harbour as it drained. I climbed out and backed the van down with the trailer. We were going to have to time this really well! I stopped the trailer just at the end of the concrete. Not all the surges were coming to the same level so we were trying to pick the biggest surge to give it a go. Cotty circled outside the harbour, jumping waves, trying to hold position. As soon as a big surge came through, he gunned it in with it. He lined up the ski with the trailer and gave it one more burst and drove straight up onto the trailer. The water started drawing back out as I clicked the winch onto the bow and started winding. The ski was getting sucked back with it. I was fighting with the winch against the outward pull of water. The ski fell backwards off the trailer. It rested half on and half off the trailer as the water sucked out. Cotty and I got under the ski and tried to heave it on. I knew those bench presses would come in handy for something! We needed that wee old woman back to give us a hand but she was out towing somewhere else from what I heard. Another surge came through and we got the ski out.

Sometimes we have sessions like that were the sessions themselves aren't as eventful as the mission that goes with them. This day looked like it would have been the day of all days and we would have ridden the biggest waves of our lives but instead it turned into a hardcore training session. I know we may seem completely nuts at times when you read this but in order to ride big waves we have to accept the craziness that comes with it. I don't think anyone can expect to surf extreme sized waves and not have extreme conditions surrounding them.

december 1st 2007

I HAD BEEN MONITORING the formation of a new swell out in the Atlantic for a couple of days. I had been speaking to Cotty about it as it was looking like the biggest we had ever seen as early forecasts were in the 13metre range. Some of you might not understand how we can predict the size of the waves, almost to the hour so let me explain. There are some very intelligent people who have studied the weather systems and translated their findings into models for Ocean users. It used to be that surfers only had the weather report on the radio or television to go by but in the last few years things have really changed with forecasting conditions at sea. We use various websites which show detailed data received from wave buoys, satellites and weather stations all across the globe. The predictions come from models created based on previous patterns and are a good guide to what is coming our way. Once the swell gets closer to shore we start looking specifically at the wave buoys and the local wind forecast. The wave buoys data give us actual up to date information on the swell size, the interval between each wave and the wind. From this we can work out when the swell will make land fall and have a good idea of the quality of the swell and the winds that will be present at that time. We can predict it to the hour now for most spots.

Cotty was considering going on a trip to Madeira again only this time with Wavelength magazine and his sponsors. He wasn't sure if it was worth the gamble at Mullaghmore as the wind looked to be severe for when the swell was due to hit the coast. It is rare for a swell that appears on forecasts a week out to hold its size and generally we would get swell that is less than was predicted. However this swell continued to grow. It was Tuesday 27th November and Cotty phoned to say he was heading to Madeira. This wasn't the first time I have been the only one thinking conditions will hold. I suppose I'm a little more optimistic than most people and I will take a gamble just in case rather than miss out. I had a feeling this was going to be the biggest one we have ever seen and I was willing to take the gamble of being at Mullaghmore in case there was a window in the wind to let me have a go at riding a few. The swell was definitely a Mullaghmore swell. There was no chance of anywhere else being able to handle the hurricane force winds with swell that size. Mullaghmore has a bump on the headland which deflects some of the wind so even on the wildest days it can sometimes be possible to sneak onto a few big ones out there. The thing is, if you aren't there, then you can't have a go if the opportunity arises.

I was now partner-less. I hate that feeling where I'm so excited and so driven to do something yet I'm held back because I need someone to play with me! As soon as Cotty told me he wasn't coming I got straight on the phone to Duncan Scott. At this stage I had towed with Duncan a number of times when Cotty couldn't make it or if Duncan didn't have a partner we would let him hitch hike with us. At that time he was the only other surfer I felt safe with in huge seas, other than Cotty. Duncan doesn't have a permanent partner .Although he has committed to tow surfing by purchasing a ski, he mainly hitches rides with other teams wherever he may be but has never committed to one person outright. That might be so that he is never let down and can always fit into the mix with whatever is going on. He rarely misses a good swell unless there is a major hold up in his life. I knew that Duncan was my only chance at riding this swell and if he wasn't able to make it then I would have to let this one go.

I called him. I told him the scenario and he was actually watching the same swell but everyone he spoke to thought it was going to be unrideable, due to the wind. He was obviously keen to surf so I told him I wanted to tow it and that I was sure that the small three hour window on Saturday morning, where the wind forecast appeared to be holding true at 18knots from the south west, was going to materialise before the storm would go nuts. I knew there was a lot of risk in making this call but we both knew this was a giant swell and agreed that Duncan should take the risk and fly over. He boarded a flight that night.

We spent the next two days watching the swell on the net, monitoring its movements through the Atlantic. It was still holding its size in fact it had risen to a massive 14.4 metres at 16 second intervals on the predictions! This was a massive swell! Mullaghmore usually starts to be big enough to break at around 5metres and you will get wave faces of 20 foot plus from a swell that big with a decent interval between the waves of about 14 seconds. You might be thinking how can a 5m swell create a wave face so much bigger? Well it is because although the swell is 5m it will decrease in size as it gets closer to the coast but when it actually hits the reef and begins to break, the wave draws water off the reef increasing the size of its face to twice the size of the swell and sometimes more, depending on the spot. So it didn't take a rocket scientist to do the maths on this one. There was no doubt that this was going to be a significant day in Irish Surfing if we actually got to ride a few.

We got the equipment ready on Friday morning and headed off to Mullaghmore. We knew it wasn't going to be possible to paddle into any of these waves as the swell was going to be so big and the wind so strong so we didn't load the big wave guns this time and only the tow surf kit.

Let me explain what I mean about kit. This isn't like getting a board from your garage, throwing it in the car and heading to the beach. Tow surfing is a mission from the word GO!. I have a long wheel base van. It gets loaded with so much crap it's unbelievable. It's a bit like when you go on holiday for the weekend and you bring a bag that is packed with enough clothes for a month knowing full well that you will never change your under pants more than once let alone wear a dinner jacket, shorts, 3 pairs of jeans, 2 pairs of shoes and two coats. But, if you didn't have 2 spare t shirts you can be sure you will spill your dinner down the front of the only one you have! That's like tow surfing! I've learned to bring absolutely everything so that in any eventuality I have a spare. That involves wetsuits, spare boards, spare foot straps, screws and fins for the boards, resin repair kits in case I damage boards. It involves extra straps for tying down the seats of the ski (we modify the basic jet ski so that it has straps across the seats to hold them on in case it gets rolled, skis are designed for fair weather use not for worst weather use! So we adapt them a little). I bring spare light boards for the trailer, spare wheel bearings, grease for the wheels, spare tires, spare life jackets, spare ski batteries, spare ropes, anchor, spare tools, really I could list so much stuff that rarely gets used but every now and again, something is needed. I remember one time my brother and I had changed the wheel bearings on the ski trailer but over tightened the nuts on them. I got about 300yrds down the country lane, where I keep my ski, before the right hand wheel over took me on the road! Both wheel bearings had broken, the ski and trailer ended up on the road and then it got lifted by a forklift back into the yard where I was lucky enough to have enough spare parts to have them fixed properly! Seriously, you would never dream of both bearings going at once but with tow surfing, anything is possible!

Duncan and I went for a warm up session on Friday afternoon as the swell was starting to show. This allowed us to make sure our hand signals and pick ups were the same and it blew the jitters out of us.

There was a definite buzz about this swell. I had a phone call that evening from Owen Conlan, a journalist from The Sun Newspaper. Owen has printed some photos of me in the past and as the forecast storm was all over the news, he wanted to know if I was going to attempt to ride it. The swell was drawing the attention of not only surfers but the public itself. My phone was ringing off the hook with friends and family wishing me luck, telling me to be safe and sending texts as they were concerned for me and wanting to know that I come back safe. You have to remember big wave surfing in Ireland was still fairly under the radar at this point and not really recognised by the general public…yet! I started to think this was going to be super sized and all the hype around it before it had even happened was unusual to say the least. I don't say to anyone if I'm going out in big surf, it happens so quickly that I don't really have a chance to call people anyway. This was different as this storm had shown on the charts a long time out and had actually deepened in strength. I was shocked at how many people were calling me. There were weather warnings all over the country and the coast guard had warnings all along the coast. One Radio article even had a man warning people to stay in doors and not to consider surfing on Saturday. I have heard these warnings before but this was different, there was a real fear in the air of what was about to smash into the west coast in the morning.

As it turned out Ritchie Fitzgerald and Gabe Davies were filming their big budget film 'Waveriders' and although they had already wrapped it up, this swell came on the last day of filming so they wanted to have it as the finale to their film. They had a massive film crew with them who were hiring out boats to sit in the channel and film from.

I didn't sleep that night. I was lying still in bed listening for the wind. Do you know when you're in bed and you hear a noise down stairs, you lie there silently and still, moving only your eye balls so as to make sure what the noise was? Well that's what I was doing. I was trying to hear if the storm had arrived.

I got up early. I remember standing in the foyer of the hotel at 6am in the dark looking at the harbour. The wind was already picking up. Usually at Mullaghmore if the harbour is choppy with the wind blowing on it then it is a good sign as the surf spot is on the other side of the headland and will therefore be in a wind shadow to some degree. Duncan and I drove round to take a look from the road.

We peered out into the inky darkness and could see mountains of white water all over the headland. There was no doubt about it, even in the dark it was obvious that the swell was Giant and the wind was holding a good direction.

We watched for about 15 minutes before Gabe and Ritchie rolled up in their van. It was getting brighter all the time. They pulled up beside the passenger side window, blocking the empty road and began watching. There was silence for about 30 seconds before they rolled the window down and said "sham it looks huge, how big do reckon it is out there?" We all ummed and ahhed for a couple of seconds as no one really wanted to commit to saying what all four of us were really thinking. "I reckon it's about 60 foot on the face out there on the sets" I said. Everyone looked at me as I said that and then looked away without saying anything. I think we all already knew that to be honest, they just wanted to see if we thought the same!

Duncan and I were ready to go. We knew we didn't have long to do this as the conditions were barely holding and we reckoned that by 11am it would be so violent out there that we would be forced back onshore.

We dropped the ski down the slip, set up and launched before it was even fully bright. Gabe and Ritchie's camera crew were buzzing around in a panic as Duncan and I drove out the harbour mouth.

As we rounded the harbour wall, I saw a wave break completely over it. I had never seen this happen before. You can get a wee bit of white water blown over it from time to time but this was a full on wave. It washed over the 25 foot wall like it was a kerb on the road. I remember thinking "this is going to be massive" I also remember thinking that size is relative and what seems 'massive' to me, might seem normal to someone in Hawaii or Mavericks...we kept heading out to sea. When you turn around the harbour wall you begin to take the swell on the bow of the ski. This is the time that I usually begin imagining what is actually out there. My mind runs wild and I envisage the most horrific sized waves and begin to doubt my ability and question myself. It's the same as when I surfed Mavericks the first time. The fear still comes up every time, to varying degrees. It's just something I've learned to deal with and accept. I think if you go out there and don't expect to be scared then you are in for a shock.

As we made our way out to the peak of the wave, right out the back. It was clear to me that these were the biggest waves I had ever been in. Huge flawless peaks were stacking on the reef, drawing tonnes of water from it and then pouring out into massive, dark cavernous tubes of death! We watched a few sets breaking and we were hooting like we had just won the lottery! It was amazing to watch these perfect, beautiful waves detonating one after another. Even as I write this I can still picture one of them stacked up on the reef as we perched on top of its shoulder looking down and into the massive pit. It was incredible. I couldn't believe Cotty wasn't there!

I heard the engine off another ski and when I turned round it was Ritchie and Gabe arriving out to the channel with their crew coming behind in a rib. The very first thing I noticed as they arrived out was the wetsuit Ritchie was wearing was identical to Duncan's. They were both sponsored by Oneill Wetsuits, a Californian brand, at the time. Oneill had made a few white suits for some of its riders. It made them look like the storm troopers from Star Wars and this was quite fitting for this occasion!

Gabe and Ritchie began towing on a few smaller insiders to warm up. I knew we didn't have time to warm up and this swell wasn't going to tolerate us taking our time. We had a window of a few hours before it sent us home and Duncan and I were only interested in riding as big as we could. We headed out to the peak of the reef, where the waves first break on the ledge. It is the same spot on the reef where Cotty and I lost the ski. No one had ridden a proper wave yet and until someone did we weren't going to be able to put a size on how big these waves really were on this day. Duncan said he would tow me first. We ended up miss timing a few waves, probably because the swell was so big and moving so quickly that we couldn't get onto them. I asked Duncan to swap with me and I'd have a go putting him onto one. Duncan is a good surfer, anyone will tell you that but in big waves he excels and surfs with style and grace. I threw him the rope and pulled him up to his feet.

A set appeared on the horizon. These sets were massive; they were coming out of a black sky and sea. They marched in from the Atlantic and filled the whole of Donegal Bay making it appear more like a bath tub than part of the ocean. As the first big set approached, I drove the ski at speed towards the second one in the set. We always try not to go on the first wave in a set in case one of us falls and then has to deal with the whole set on the head. It is safer to choose the last one if possible but we also want to ride the biggest so sometimes have to take the risk of maybe falling early in a set and facing another four or five waves on the head.

I drove in parallel to the wave. I glanced back at Duncan on the rope and gave him a nod, he lifted one thumb from the rope handle and that was enough for me to know he was ok to go. I banked the ski around on its left side and began whipping Duncan round behind me on the rope so as to position him onto the peak of the wave. It was a frighteningly big wave. At this point I was now standing on the ski driving at about 16mph towards shore, about half a mile out and lined up with my marker point on land. Duncan was on the rope, strapped into his board. Behind was a huge stacking wall of water which was lined up for about 400 yards to our left and to our right. It hadn't broken yet. At this point I could see that Duncan was looking extremely small in front of this stacking charcoal coloured, liquid mountain. I slowed the ski down a little to let the wave get closer to us and begin to pick us up. I then gave the ski one last squirt of gas and flung him into the peak as it stood vertical on the reef. Duncan disappeared down the face of it as I pulled the ski up over the unbroken shoulder. The section he was on detonated sending plumes of water up into the air. All I could see was the back of the wave which looked to be around 25-30 feet in height. I was pretty sure Duncan was riding a 55-60foot wave just in front of me. I drove at speed behind the wave looking and searching for him in the aftermath in case he fell. This is one of the worrying things out there. You don't know if your partner has fallen and you have to be vigilant at all times until you see him kick out clear into the channel. He did just that. I drove in to get him at the end of his ride and he was stoked. He looked a little shocked to be honest but as he climbed on to the sled he reached up and gave me 5! As we drove back out to the peak, he shouted to me over the sound of the engine, full of excitement about the wave and gagging to tell me about what he had just ridden and seemed to be in disbelief as to the shear size and volume of the waves.

We switched and I took the rope again. We felt like we were in sync with each other and the swell! We had found our flow and Duncan was now ready to put me onto one.

I slid off the ski and let him take the helm. As I slipped my feet into my straps and took the end of the rope, I remember not feeling any nerves. I didn't feel that fear I normally get just before my first wave of a session. I shouted to Duncan the same thing I say every session to Cotty "Just put me on a bomb! Wait it out and just put me on a F£$kin bomb!" I am only interested in the big ones and believe it or not I think it is safer to ride a huge one out there than go chasing after mediocre waves. It is best to wait for the monsters to come through, watch one as it approaches and then put the surfer onto it. I think its best as you can see it coming, you can watch it move around as it approaches the reef and you can safely, well relatively, place the surfer where he needs to be. This is much safer than getting the surfer on the rope and driving round like a headless chicken, hunting down anything that wants to break. I have learned that it's best to leave the small ones and let them go. Even if I am scared of the big ones, it doesn't pay to go on a small one and risk falling and getting cleaned up by a bigger one that follows. I completely believe it's safer to go on a big one. Some of you reading this might think I'm F£$kin nuts but believe me it makes sense. Being out in that environment becomes more possible through learning little pieces of knowledge that may seem completely crazy to onlookers but makes us feel more comfortable. I just laughed out loud there as I read what I just wrote, yeah that does sound crazy actually. I've just told you that it's safer to ride a huge wave than a small one! I completely understand if you have no idea what I'm talking about and if you think I'm crazy, I'm really not. Most of us aren't! Craziness is only relative anyway!

Duncan was standing on the ski with his legs astride the seat to get the best view over the lines of swell towards the horizon. "Al, we're on! there's a f$%^in monster coming!" he yelled. He was kind of looking at the wave approaching with one eye whilst looking over his shoulder with the other so I could hear his voice in the wind. "I'll get you up" he said. "Clear?" he asked. We use the word clear instead of go, no or yes so there is no confusion in what is being said. If everything is ok then the partner responds with the same word. I shouted back "Clear!" He fired up the ski, took up the slack in the rope and then accelerated pulling me up out of the water and onto my feet. Now I could see what he was talking about! There was no doubt that the wave coming was a monster. It was coming out of the black ocean beneath a lightening forked angry sky. It had my name on it. I remember tilting my head back and closing my eyes momentarily and thinking of my Dad before focusing on the wave. I don't know why I did that. Duncan shouts over the engine noise "You want it?" I replied with one word which I shouted back to him "Yeah". That one word or a nod between us communicates so much. It tells Duncan or whoever might be driving that I trust them to put me in safely to the wave, I trust that they will be there if I fall and that they will do whatever it takes to get me out of trouble should something go wrong.

The sun came out momentarily just as Duncan began his approach on the ski. He accelerated towards the wave in a parallel direction and then banked around to his left and lined us up with the mark up on land. The wave was massive! I remember thinking "Holy F$%k this is huge!" I felt small and insignificant. I didn't feel scared for some reason just amping to get on it. I faded out to the right hand side of the wake as Duncan gave the ski its last squirt of gas to propel me into the towering peak. I dropped the rope and began to glide into position as Duncan pulled away at speed and the wave stood like a 6 storey office block. As I got to about half way down it, it just lurched on the reef and grew massively above me. I thought I was a goner. It tried to suck me up the face with it and I felt like I wasn't going to be able to make the rest of the drop. For a split second I envisaged myself landing on my back on the face of the wave and getting sucked up over the falls. I snapped out of it! I tightened down into a low crouch and took the rock boils at high speed. My board chattered off the surface of the wave and the boils. I made it out to the channel without falling! I was so f£$%in stoked! I was going nuts! I couldn't calm down I was so excited, I mean ecstatic, I was squealing like a girl! Sometimes the ride is so intense that it is difficult to absorb all the action whilst on it and it isn't until after it that the full feeling kicks in and I can relive the ride in my head. It is a mix of excitement and relief and I suppose it comes from being so close to disaster but riding out of it and into safety that keeps me hooked. Duncan came in and got me on the ski. Ritchie drove up and said "Sham, that was nuts, I was scared for you big man!" He looked shocked. He said "I've never seen you look so small!" Duncan and I were high fiving and hugging completely loving the moment! It was a great feeling.

We all rode some more waves that day. Gabe went on the end section of one that was frightening as it stood really tall behind him as he bottom turned around the section before covering him in spray. Ritchie went on a big thick one that shut down behind him driving him deep into the only wipe out of the session. He later told me he could see the rock ledge under water! He got hit really hard and he must have been pretty deep even with two impact vests on! There was a definite threatening feel to the surf that day and we all knew that one mistake could have horrific consequences. We were forced ashore by raging winds and hail stones at 11am. I didn't realise until we were heading back to the harbour that the headland was packed with people and cars all watching us out there. Normally we might see one or two people drive round the isolated headland but it turned out that people had actually driven from all over the place to see us surf that day. To my amazement we met a guy called Justin Avery, an Australian living in London. He heard from his friend in Ireland that some surfers were going to have a go at riding this swell. He boarded a plane and drove through the night, slept in his car and then filmed the session!

Duncan and I were buzzing! I knew it was a big session but I didn't realise how big until we saw the photographs! Even we were in shock as to what had just gone down. All our phones were ringing hot with friends and family checking to see if we were back in and more importantly to find out how big it was. Journalists were ringing us from all over the world for interviews and photos.

The next day photos and quotes from us were printed in newspapers all over the country. International websites were running stuff too. We were getting emails from other tow surfers in Hawaii and California congratulating us. It was crazy! We made BBC World News, BBC Radio one, The Times, The Sun, the list goes on and on. It was unreal. We spent the next week doing multiple interviews daily for radio stations, websites, magazines and newspapers. It was like all of a sudden not only did the surfing world know that big waves existed in Ireland and that a handful of people are riding them but also the general public were seeing it in their homes and in their newspapers. Cotty was getting texts and calls from his mates saying "Al is all over the news for riding 60 footers!" He couldn't believe it and phoned me from Madeira to hear if it was true. He was stoked for us but also gutted that he missed it though I'm sure he was having a fun trip in Madeira as the same swell was travelling through the Atlantic en route to him.

The Coleraine Chronicle and the Coleraine Times ran a story and some photos later in the week. A local man from Castlerock came and spoke to me about the article. I remember when he first saw photos of me riding waves at Mavericks that he commented "You don't get waves like that in this country!" I replied at the time with "You do, I'll prove it someday!" At the time he obviously thought I didn't know what I was talking about but now he knows differently!

Shortly after the swell we heard on the news that the swell was the biggest ever recorded swell in Irish Waters.

The waves we rode were recognised by The Billabong XXL competition again only this year we stood more of a chance of doing well as some of the rides appeared to be contenders in The Biggest Wave Category. We were invited over to Anaheim California by Bill Sharp and Sam George for the awards ceremony in April. I had recently returned from another trip to Mavericks but I thought that the expense of going back over to the states was worth paying for as I don't think a surfer from the UK or Ireland had ever been invited to that. We had numerous entries in the competition before, as did a couple of other guys in particular from the first big session we all had at Aileen's but I don't think anyone had been invited over to the awards before so we were quite surprised. We sat in a packed auditorium amongst some of the best big wave riders in the world, media and surf industry representatives. On the big screen behind the stage they played what they call 'The year in review'. The show started with Hawaiian Big Wave Rider Garrett McNamara navigating his way through a mutant giant wave at a reef called Teahupoo, in Tahiti. It then went through sessions in Tasmania, South Africa and then onto us! People were hooting and whistling like they were for the other rides they had just seen and our rides and waves looked like they were definitely fit to be in the mix! It gave me goose bumps all over me. I don't do this for recognition nor for praise but it was definitely a good feeling seeing how far we had come in such a short space of time.

Just after the action packed video, Mark Occhilupo, former ASP World Champion walked onto the stage as the MC for the evening. He began to speak to the crowd and then out of nowhere said "I'd like to congratulate Alastair, Duncan and Andrew for bringing Irish Surfing to the world stage!" We were in shock! Up on stage was one of surfing biggest idols, achievers and one of the world's best surfers. Not only were we in a room packed with elite big wave riders and athletes but we had just been publically addressed by Occy! This was an amazing feeling! I was so stoked!

I know Duncan, Cotty and I rode the waves but it was the photographers that made it possible for us to be included in this awards show. It was a great feeling and I know everyone of us felt stoked that what we love doing at home had been recognised by the very people who introduced big wave riding to us through photos and videos. It was a great feeling.

None of us won any of the categories. The ride of the year went to Hawaiian, Shane Dorian for a death defying ride in Tahiti. We didn't expect to win, we knew lots of the other waves in the event were way more impressive than ours but to have been worthy of being in the mix was enough for us to feel good!

This wasn't all that was spawned from December 1st 2007. People had begun to search for us on the net. It wasn't long before we had invites to compete in The APT (Association of Professional Tow Surfers) World Tow in Championships in Chile and also to The Nelscott Reef Tow In Classic in Oregon, USA.

This was unbelievable. I was asked by the organiser of the Oregon contest, John Forse, who my partner would be for the contest. He had obviously seen photos of Duncan and I towing. I wished that both Cotty and Duncan could partner with me as I felt Cotty was my partner but Duncan stepped in when Cotty couldn't make it. Cotty wasn't giving up on tow surfing, far from it. He still wanted it more than anything. I knew without a doubt what to decide but I didn't want to hurt Duncan's feelings and wished that I could put his name forward too in some way. Cotty and I were the team, we committed to each other a long time ago. I was not going to break that bond over one session. When Cotty saw the photos of December 1st, he described it as "It was like someone having it off with my missus and then splashing it all over the tabloids!" Cotty and I had already achieved so much and I knew that Duncan hadn't committed to anyone in particular. I really didn't know what to say to Duncan, I felt really awkward. I didn't want to hurt his feelings and I didn't want him to think I was unappreciative for him stepping in but I knew Cotty and I were a team. It felt like the Carl and Cotty situation only there was way more involved at this stage. It was a difficult time. I imagine it's what a married woman feels when she finds out her husband has just had the ride of his life on another woman!

Right: **Eric Akiskalian bottom turns on a Chilean Beast.**
Photo: www.robkeithphotography.com

the apt world cup tow in championships 2008, pichilemu, chile

THIS WAS OUR FIRST International invite. It came through our friend Eric Akiskalian at www.towsurfer.com who also ran The APT (Association of Professional Tow Surfers) with Rodney Kilborn. Eric has an amazing passion to push the sport to new levels through participating in it and also supporting all the guys involved. He also developed a series of big wave events in various locations around the globe to which a select list of international big wave surfers were invited. He put it out for a team to represent our region and it ended up that Cotty and I were put forward as most suitable candidates. We were stoked.

This was an amazing honour to been invited to compete in this event. When the organisers did their press release listing all the 24 international invited teams it was enough to make us shake in our booties! Names like

Garret McNamara, Grant Baker, Tyler Fox. All guys who had numerous big wave achievements and accolades to their names. We were only invited as alternates. Basically there were a list of 24 teams as main list invitees and then a list of eight other teams who would be called upon if one of the main teams couldn't make it. So we were hoping that the short notice of 48 hours to get to Chile was going to be difficult for one of the teams. The way it would work was that the organisers had allocated a three month waiting period within which time they would give all the competitors 48 hours notice to be at the contest site ready to compete. As I'm sure you can imagine, that meant for three months, we were glued to our emails and phones waiting to hear if the swell was big enough for Eric to make the call. They would only make the call if the surf was going to be in the 40 foot face height range. There were a couple of times when they thought conditions would be right and they put us all on standby but at the last minute the wind changed and they couldn't call it 'On'.

The swell didn't materialise during the three month holding period so Eric and Rodney agreed with the local council, the sponsors and the competitors to extend the holding period in the hope of a good swell. It must be a very difficult and frustrating event to organise when you have

Eric Akiskalian, Flecha Escobar and Keith Galbraith at Punta de Lobos.
Photo: www.towsurfer.com

so many sponsors etc all so keen for the event to run but the Ocean doesn't serve up the goods. I know it must be difficult to explain to businesses that the event can't run until the waves turn up!

It wasn't until October 2008 that a potential swell showed up. I have a phone that allows me to read my emails. It was 12:10am on Sunday night and I was in bed in my house, in Portrush. I had my phone on silent but I noticed a red flashing light reflecting off the white ceiling as I tried to sleep. I knew that meant I probably had either an email or a text message on my phone so I rolled over and lifted it off the floor. It was an email. I assumed it was just a random marketing email from a teeth whitening company or something but to my amazement, it was from Eric. It said "contest is running, Wednesday, you guys are in the event!" That's all it said. If you remember when I asked Eric for tow board advice he also sent a one liner then too but I didn't ask for anymore information at that time. This time I needed to be sure that he sent that email to the right person and if he meant that someone had dropped out of the event and he was putting us in their place. I emailed right back and asked "Are you serious? Are we definitely in the contest?" Within seconds he responded with "YES YES YES!!!!! YOU'RE IN!"

I immediately phoned cotty, who was also in bed sleeping. "Alright mate?" he asked me as he answered the phone, obviously wondering why I was phoning him so late. I blurted out "Chile has just got the green light and we're in!." "You what?" He replied. I explained to him what I'd just got in emails and he gradually began to understand what I was talking about. We both got out of our beds and got onto the net to start looking at flights. I emailed Eric and confirmed we would be there. Three hours and £1600 later we were booked on flights to Santiago Chile leaving the next day via Paris! It is so expensive to travel last minute but we had no choice. If we wanted to do it then we had to pay it. We both figured it would be worth spending that money for the experience and we knew that we would come away with a ranking in an international contest.

We spent the next day packing and organising everything at home before we left. Cotty cancelled plumbing and lifeguarding jobs and I moved site meetings back to the following week when we would return.

Arriving in Chile was interesting. We thought we were supposed to be getting on a coach organised by the event for the competitors but there was some sort of mistake and no coach showed up so we hired a car. We didn't go to a normal car hire desk we rented from some random guy on the footpath at the airport. I don't know what came over us! We went in his car to his little office, paid him cash and took the car. It was a very strange set up but nonetheless we headed off on the three hour drive to Punta de Lobos, Pichilemu.

We arrived at Pichilemu and noticed that it was fairly deserted as it appeared to be a summer resort and as this was winter, it was pretty well closed down. We found the headland that the big wave spot broke off. It has two very unique sandy coloured rocks which stand out on the edge of the reef. There were waves but it wasn't Giant yet. We knew it was due to arrive during the night so we weren't too concerned about that. We met up with Eric and then went off to check into our accommodation.

I'm sure if you are a surfer then you will have heard of Koby Abberton. He needs no introduction. We bumped into him in the car park of the rental accommodation. He was with another guy who we assumed was his tow partner. "Do you guys wanna share a house?" he asked in a strong Aussie accent. Cotty and I looked at each other and said "Yeah why not?" We all shook hands and introduced ourselves and checked into a house for the duration of the event. Koby and his tow partner Ryan Hipwood were one of a couple of Aussie Teams invited.

That night a competitors meeting was called in the nearby restaurant. We met up there with guys we knew from previous trips or sessions else where like Carlos Burle, Grant Baker etc…The room was packed full of surfers from all over the globe. Not just any surfers, these guys were at the forefront of big wave riding across the globe. Some of them were international super stars like Carlos or Koby and some were less well known. Nevertheless the contest was packed with surfers dedicated to riding big waves all of whom were there to compete for the title of APT World Tow In Cup Champion and earn a place in the next event on the tour on Maui. The meeting was about the contest format which was largely being debated by the surfers so as to decide upon and agree a suitable format depending on the conditions. Local Chilean surfer Ramon, reckoned the swell forecast was running a day late and that the event will not run until Thursday. Cotty and I didn't get involved in the debate about format. We left that to other more qualified surfers to decide. Most of the guys had competed before in big waves so their views were valid, we didn't think ours were worth much so we just kept our mouths shut and listened to what everyone else was saying.

Eventually it was agreed that Wednesday would be spent meeting at the judging podium (which was being erected over night by the organisers crew) every three hours in case the swell was sufficient to run a few heats off before the full brunt arrived on Thursday. It was agreed that each team would surf one 40 minute heat in which each surfer must ride at least two waves and drive the ski for his partner to ride two waves. The heats would consist of 4 teams which all rotated on a priority system. So when the team with priority chose to ride a wave, the next team in line would move up the priority queue and they would have their choice of whatever wave they wanted and no one else could go on it if they wanted it. If someone interfered with that rule or broke it, then their team would be penalised.

So basically each surfer had to ride two waves per heat to progress and the scores would be tallied and added to the other surfers score and then the top two teams would progress to the next round. There were 16 teams in total out of a possible 24, some of which couldn't make it at such short notice. It probably sounds a bit chaotic or maybe I'm not explaining it very clearly.

The next day we went to the podium every three hours to check the conditions. I noticed how the conditions reminded me off home a little. In particular it reminded me of Mullaghmore the way the swell wrapped around the exposed headland although the rocks and coast were more dusty and golden in colour compared to the dark slabs of rock sticking out into the water at Mullaghmore. The contest didn't go ahead that day but the swell did pick up and the spot started to break. The organisers let us

This is me taking Brazilian Carlos Burle, Tom Kay and my friend from America Ernie Capbert for a surf at G-spot.
Photo: **Kelly Allen**

use the skis to go and have a practice session and get a feel for the spot. You might have been wondering how we were going to surf in a tow in contest without bringing a ski with us. The organisers had arranged all the skis so competitors didn't need to.

We suited up and drove out. Conditions were windy, a lot of guys were complaining about it but we were used to that sort of surf. We rarely get a glassy smooth day at home in big surf so this was kind of normal to us. The surf wasn't massive, maybe a couple of 20 foot faces coming through which was obviously the start of the swell due to come in over night.

We were used to surfing in big waves on our own. We rarely had anyone in the water with us when it was big, certainly not a bunch of the best, most experienced big wave riders in the world. There was a real energy in the air as teams zipped in and out of the impact zone firing each other onto set waves as they stacked on the headland. I remember seeing Brazilian Carlos Burle going on the biggest one of the afternoon, looking solid and comfortable as the waves stood in front of the rocky outcrop. I know Carlos from taking him surfing at an offshore spot in Bundoran, some years ago and also from being at the XXL Awards in California earlier in the year. The big

Californians Chuck Patterson and Scott Chandler looked like super heroes out there. Both guys are huge but Chuck in particular looks like a gladiator standing at around 6'3" tall with muscles stacked on his huge frame. Cotty and I struggled to get waves to be honest. All the guys were going for it. We were being a little too polite I think as we were used to being on our own. We were getting really frustrated not getting any waves but I suppose we were out classed and this was normal. We just couldn't find a rhythm to get onto a few. Every time we went for one someone else would be deeper on the wave and we would just let them go. It ended up that we needed to be more aggressive and just take the attitude of 'We are going, don't get in the f£$kin way!' We did get a few waves each and then went back to shore to let one of the other teams go for a warm up.

The morning of the contest was very different to the afternoon before. The waves were much cleaner and the sets were much bigger although a little infrequent. This is the first time Koby really started to come alive. Up until this point he seemed to stay calm and relaxed and kept himself to himself. As soon as the surf was showing on the headland with proper sets coming through, he was amping. Cotty, Koby, Ryan and I stood and watched the waves break on the headland while Koby talked through ideas for setting his game plan. A crowd of spectators from all over Chile were beginning to gather on the headland in the hope of seeing some big waves being ridden

Cotty and I were in heat four of the event which meant we got to watch the first few heats to see what the other guys were doing. As you know I have competed a lot in the past in small wave contests but Cotty hadn't really done that much competing. Cotty was a little concerned as to how he would fare in a contest situation. I suppose we both knew what to expect in some ways and in others we were trying to work it out as we went along.

Grant 'Twiggy' Baker was down a partner so he paired up with Reinaldo IBarra in the first heat. Within minutes he put him onto a bomb that drained the water off the inside ledge exposing the rock. Reinaldo pulled into a big tube disappearing from view for a few seconds before being spat out the end of the wave. The crowd watching hooted and whistled towards the surf! The contest was ON!

We watched a few more waves get ridden and then went to the launch site to get suited and booted ready for our heat. The water was cold like home, so we saw this as an advantage over some of the guys but we knew that we were competing against a crew of super charged surfers and it was going to take more than a little bit of cold to hinder their performance.

We warmed up on the beach which was tucked behind the headland and was somewhat protected from the big 30ft sets busting on the point. We put on our coloured vests. Each team wears a particular colour of vest so the judges can tell what team is surfing. In our case, we wore white. We were up against three other teams from Chile, Brazil and Australia. The Australian team consisted of eight time world champion paddler Jamie Mitchell and the big lunged Mark Vissor. I say big lunged as he has a video on the net where he lies on the bottom of a swimming pool for 1 minute 30 seconds after he blows all his air out. Yes, I said after he blows his air out. Then, before surfacing, does a 50 metre swim!

Cotty and I shook hands and slapped each other a few times before going down to get on the ski. We agreed that we would wait for the big ones as normal. We decided that we would each surf for 15 minutes allowing 10 minutes extra in case we have any mishaps like one of us doesn't get any good ones, or we lose a board or something.

I towed Cotty first as normal. We were fourth in the priority system so we didn't have first dibs at the big ones so while the other three teams waited on the sets I made the most of the time and fired Cotty onto a few average ones. One of which I must admit was terrible wave selection on my part. I put Cotty onto one that was walled up too far down the line and although I was trying to put him into a tube like Twiggy had done for his partner earlier, there was slim chance of him making it out of it. He went anyway, pulled into the barrel but it closed down on him sending him over the dry rocks. He was getting washed around the big round rock by waves in the rest of the set which just happened to be bigger! I had to let a few waves hit him as I couldn't get the ski in until they passed. A big one was charging down the point with Vissor riding it, I knew I had to get him before this one or he might get hurt if he wasn't already. I zipped in grabbed his hand and pulled him on just before Vissor got trapped by a closing section on the wave and sent into the same place I had just got Cotty from. I gunned the ski and raced into the deep water.

We headed straight back out as Jamie swooped in and pulled Vissor onto the sled. Cotty was up and now we had priority. Everyone else had ridden out their priority so we now had choice of what we wanted. I waited it out, and then put Cotty on a big peaking wave way out the back. I watched the wave from the back as he rode it and I could see he managed to get a big carve in on time before the wave got to the shallow section of the reef. I couldn't see him but I could see his trail of white water from his board coming over the back of the wave so I knew he was still up and riding as he entered into the sketchy section. He rode through

This is me during the APT World Tow In Cup Championship at Punta do Lobos, Pichelimu, Chile 2008. *Photo:* Tim Ditty

the churned up bumpy base of the wave as the curl through over him. He then managed to throw in another few carves before the wave petered out into deep water. We were pretty sure that was a high scoring wave. He rode one more which wasn't as big but made it right through to the inside again before we swapped.

I didn't fall on any thanks to Cottys' good driving and I rode one similar to the big one he got although I didn't go as close to the rocks as he did. There is a photo of me on a wave taken from the safety boat in the channel.

It shows me right next to the completely dry rocks with the wave behind me. It was these rocks that Cotty was washed over. We were lucky though; some of the guys that fell in there didn't get back out to surf and had to give up.

We didn't make it through to the semi finals but the Aussies did. We were stoked for them. We saw them get a couple of bombs and the local Chilean team also made it through. The local team were playing with the waves! They just looked so relaxed and comfortable out there, obviously they knew it so well.

The teams that made it into the top eight which was the semi finalists all were guaranteed a spot in the next contest on Maui at the famous break called Jaws. We ended up tenth over all which we were absolutely stoked about! Koby and Ryan ended up victorious and took home the title!

Cotty and I were so happy, we had come from surfing on our own off the west coast of Ireland to finishing tenth in this international event amongst a field of experienced big wave super stars. I cried on the way back to the airport as I remembered when I won the British Student Nationals and phoning home and my Dad being so excited. I know we didn't win this event, far from it, but finishing tenth was enough for us to feel like we had achieved something and I really wish my Dad could have been here to see that. The last thing Dad knew of me was that I wanted to go and surf mavericks, it would be great for him to see what I've been up to since.

Later that year we received invites to events in The Canary Islands, Spain, Oahu and we also made it into the Jaws contest. This time we were on all the main invitee lists as opposed to the alternate lists. I think the fact that we were willing to drop everything at the drop of a hat, spend huge amounts of money and travel to Chile combined with seeing video and stills of us surfing was enough for the organisers of the events to warrant inviting us.

When I was young, the only big wave contest in the world, that I was aware of anyway, was The Eddie. It was a contest in memory of Legendary Hawaiian Surfer Eddie Aikau. It is held at Waimea bay on Oahu. We hadn't been invited to that one although I had been fortunate enough to make the nomination list a couple of times.

gotta take the rough with the smooth

"THE CONTEST IS ON boys!, get here in 48 hours!" read the email, this time from Nelscott Reef Tow In Classic Organiser, John Forse. This was familiar now and we swung into action and booked flights.

I was to fly to Heathrow and meet with Cotty and then we were to fly together to Portland! This was the first time the short notice really caused us problems!

I checked in for my flight from Belfast on a thick foggy morning. The flight was delayed by 90 minutes! By chance Ritchie and his wife Briohny were also on the same flight en route for a connecting flight to Sydney. We were all highly stressed as we eventually landed in Heathrow. As I waited for my boards, they legged it to the next terminal and made their flight by the skin of their teeth. All the bags had been taken from the belt and I was standing on my own waiting on my boards to show up. I phoned Cotty about ten times as I waited, panicking. He was trying to keep me calm as he waited at the gate for me. "It'll be ok mate, don't worry, you'll make it! Calm down!" He reassured me. I was waiting on my bag of boards. In it I had a tow board weighing 11kgs and two 9 footers. Each team was allowed to nominate one team member to take part in the paddle event and Cotty insisted I did it, hence the paddle boards.

Eventually my boards arrived and I had 15 minutes to get from where I was through check in, security and to the gate. I knew this was going to be tight but I'm well used to everything being hectic! I started running, well if you can call dragging that board bag and my kit bag running, then that's what I was doing. Sweat was lashing off me as I made it to the underground tube train to the next terminal. It was just my luck that my connecting flight was leaving from a different terminal! I squeezed the boards onto the train as everyone stared. I don't know whether they were wondering what was in the bags or if I was about to pass out and have a heart attack! I got to the desk and the staff told me they were closed! I didn't even argue with them about letting me on as I knew that would be time wasted I just demanded they put me on the next flight. I phoned Cotty as the girl at the desk tried to source me another flight. He was like "What! Are you kidding?" I reassured him this time that everything will be ok and I will get to Portland and not to worry. I said "Just get on the flight and wait at the airport, I will call you when I turn up and we will drive to the coast together!" He settled down and got on the flight. The only flight I could get was one to Seattle which meant a three hour drive to Portland and then another three hour drive to the coast. It was leaving in two hours and I worked out that by getting this flight it would mean arriving in Lincoln City at the event site exactly six hours before the contest was due to start. Now, that might sound like crazy travelling, and yes it is but I had to do it! As the saying goes you only live once! I paid the extra money for the flight, checked in and sat down to eat a sandwich just in time to watch Cotty's plane take off without me.

When I eventually got on my flight I scored with the exit seat. The flight was fully boarded and everyone was ready for take off when the Captain came on the speaker. He told us that there was a problem with a de-icer unit on one of the wings and that it was being fixed. I immediately thought oh no! He said it would only be half an hour and we would be on our way. That left me 5hrs 30mins once I got to the contest site. I was a little concerned at this stage but it wasn't until an hour later that things began to go really pear shaped. He came back on the speaker saying that the unit needs replaced and they would be a little longer, I really started to panic. The plane was getting really hot and I was starting to get stressed out. I couldn't believe this. My first flight was delayed, I miss my connection and now the plane I'm on is broken! I started thinking maybe I wasn't supposed to be in Oregon! After a total of 2hrs 30mins the Captain announced that the plane could no longer sit on the run way as it had out stayed its time slot. He said that we would be taken off the plane put up for the night in a hotel and put on the first flight in the morning. I didn't have time for that! I was now down to 3hrs 30 minutes left of time that I had for things to go wrong before the contest would start. I was off that plane in a flash. As people waited for their hotel allocations I waited on my luggage and while I phoned airlines to try and book me onto another flight. I knew I would have needed a three hour check in time so without a doubt I was not going to make it for the start of the contest. I tried lots of airlines but there was nothing until the morning. That was it, dead in the water. I wasn't going to make it to Oregon. I booked a flight back to Belfast and I tried to call Cotty. He was half way there assuming I was coming behind him! I was so annoyed for him. I knew he was due to touch down in Michigan and I hoped that he would check his messages before flying on. I immediately started emailing John Forse so that he would know what had happened and at least get Cotty another partner. Because we usually tow surf in Ireland, I had all the kit, life vests, rope and his favourite board! It was a nightmare. I felt so bad. More so because Cotty was on his way without knowing I wasn't going than about missing the event myself.

As it turned out cotty was teamed up with Mavericks surfer, Scott Eggers for the event. The surf was pumping, huge clean waves. Cotty and Scott had never towed together before so probably had a few teething problems but they both apparently rode some great waves. I later saw the shots from the contest and I was stoked for Cotty. The one wave that stood out was a really tall big blue face with a lip throwing behind him. He was wearing a yellow competitor's jersey and riding a yellow tow board. It is a cool shot.

Although I didn't get to go, I did learn something. I learned that travelling at last minute to the other side of the world is extremely stressful! At the time I was annoyed. I wanted to do the contest but I didn't want all the stress I had been feeling. I think I was gutted to have missed such an opportunity. It felt like I had missed out on something that had come my way through hard work. It wasn't until a few weeks later that I realised how missing the event was not the end of the world. If anything it made me realise that it is surfing big waves here at home that I value so dearly. Yes I love the opportunities to travel and compete and I hope I get invited to lots more events but missing this event made me take stock and slow down.

CHAPTER 16

8000 miles, seven days, three swells, two oceans

IT'S 7:30AM ON SATURDAY, 19 October 2009. I'm one of those people that just can't lie in, even after a hectic week at work, so I'm straight up and checking my phone. During the night I've had an email from 'Nelscott Reef Tow In Classic' organiser John Forse, notifying me that the Nelscott Reef Tow in Classic has gone to amber. It's the second year running that my tow-in partner Cotty and I have been invited to the event, which has a waiting period for swell that runs from 1 October to 31 December. At any point during that time we could get 48 hours' notice that the event is on; it's not a lot of warning, but the organisers need to be sure that the swell they are watching is going to produce the goods before asking people to travel. As you know, I've had problems making this event before and I know full well the stress than can be involved in it. Cotty and I were the only Europeans invited to the event, and off all the competitors we have furthest to go. The amber alert meant that the Classic was scheduled to take place the following Wednesday; I was to expect confirmation of that on Monday.

As if this wasn't enough excitement for a Saturday morning, it looked like there was a potentially huge swell heading for one of our own big-wave spots, Aileen's. Unfortunately it was forecast to peak on the same day as the contest over in Nelscott, and as Cotty and I hadn't had a season opener yet, we were dead keen on getting in. But we knew that if it came to it, we would have to forgo a session at Aileen's to compete at Nelscott – As much as I value surfing at home more than any contest it's not every day you get invited to surf among the best big-wave surfers in the world, so getting to Oregon was a priority. So I spent the weekend getting our kit ready for both Aileen's and Nelscott, just in case we were able to fit in a ride at both.

As it turned out, on Monday morning the organisers green-lighted Nelscott for Thursday, meaning I was able to fly out after surfing Aileen's on the Tuesday. Cotty flew over on Monday night, arriving at 10:30pm. We drove for seven hours through the night, arriving at Aileen's at 5:30am, I nailed a sleeping tablet and bunked down in the back of my van under guns and tow boards for a few hours. We had stacked the guns in the van at an angle and then put all the tow boards on top of them allowing us enough space to curl up on the damp wooden floor of the van. We only had one sleeping bag between us and Cotty insisted I used it so I gave him half my clothes to wear. I woke at 8am and saw Cotty lying there, wearing all his clothes, most of mine, a life jacket and a board bag, it was hilarious! He still argues that I can't classify two hours kip as sleeping like a log…

The swell wasn't due to hit until midday, but I get anxious if I don't check it out, so we donned our boots and stomped down through the fields to get a look from the top of the cliffs. Huge, storm-driven waves were exploding on the ledge: the surf was really angry, almost out of control. We've surfed waves of all sizes here before and this looked like a tow-in job to us, although the inside rescue area between the cliffs and the break appeared more dangerous than usual. It was like a white water rapid – one mistake out here could result in either one of us being stuck on the cliffs until the swell backed off enough to let the other go in on the ski to retrieve them. The safety channel was more or less closing out, but we thought we could get away with a few rides, so set up our stuff.

I towed Cotty first. I put Cotty onto a huge one – I saw him drop down a really steep face as the wave opened up into a huge cavernous barrel behind him. He got to the bottom and looked back up at the lip as if he

Right: **This is the day the cover shot was taken. Apparently before we headed out, there was a very tense atmosphere around Cotty and I, my face says it all.**

October 2009, Doolin Harbour. *Photo:* Conn Osborne

was looking the thing straight in the eye, then navigated his way around a huge section that ended up detonating behind him and completely covering him in white water. Somehow, he emerged from it in one piece and rode out into the channel. It was one of the heaviest rides I have ever seen at Aileen's – when the white water gobbled him up I was readying myself for a rescue.

The monster Cotty put me into was definitely the bumpiest big wave I've ever ridden. When I let go of the tow-rope I faded into the peak, and the wave just stood up, growing from the base as it sucked the water off the reef. It didn't feel like I was moving down the face rather that I was being pulled backwards up it as the wave grew ever steeper. I stayed low and tight and took every bump at high speed, but never felt like I reached the bottom.

Both Cotty and I knew that it was vitally important that we got out of the water without incident that day, so after four waves each we decided to cut the session short. The swell had grown so big that waves were breaking on the slip. Paul Okane, his partner Barry and I worked as a team to recover the skis, but even so, Paul's ski ended up on the rocks twice, and Barry was bulldozed by the trailer when a wave hit him.

Next morning Cotty and I were on the 11am flight out of Belfast to Heathrow, then onto Chicago and Portland, followed by a three-hour drive to our motel in Lincoln City, Oregon. This year we both made it to the flight! Cotty managed to nab a few hours' kip in transit but, being 6'5, I have resigned myself to the discomfort of airplane seats and don't even try to get to sleep. Instead I sat and stared into space thinking about the beasts we had just ridden and the fact that we were on route to surf another swell in another ocean with some of the best big-wave riders in the world. Finally, at 1am, we checked into our motel on the edge of the beach: jet lagged, tired from travelling and surfing and starving hungry. Succumbing to sleep over hunger, we both crashed out.

Thursday morning brought super-glassy conditions, although the beach break was a nightmare to navigate on a jet ski. We had been leant a ski by a local crew in the contest. We managed to get knocked off it twice by the shore break right in front of all the spectators and the judges, very embarrassing! Nelscott breaks about a mile out to sea, and when we eventually got out there it was beautiful. Looking ashore, we could see the occasional bank of fog nestled between the mountains; when the sun broke through it reflected off the glassy ocean. The waves were solid and really consistent – the 17.5ft swell at 16 seconds had definitely shown up! I noticed how playful the wave looked, and how surfable it was. It seemed to shift between two spots on the reef and either peak out the back, or kind of wedge up on the inside and barrel.

When we surf Aileen's or Mullaghmore, we're usually thinking about what happens if we fall, and as a result we tend to surf those spots conservatively (well, relatively). We call them 'run for your life' waves – you don't want to fall if you can help it out there. By comparison, Nelscott looked fun. It didn't have the anger that we're used to seeing in a swell; it didn't look threatening or intimidating. In fact, at times I had to mentally shake myself and remember that the waves were huge; it just didn't have the big-wave feel that we're used to. It looked like we were going to be able to surf the wave and do turns on the face.

Left: **Barry, Cotty and I put Paul's ski into the water as he backs his truck down the slip.**
Photo: Conn Osborne

I usually tow Cotty in, race along on the ski and try to keep an eye on him from the shoulder, unless he goes out of view. This time I was putting him into waves and watching him throw fans of spray off the back like he was surfing a two-foot wave, not one 30 foot high! It was cool. When it was my turn, I almost didn't know what to do because I'm so used to looking at big waves like they're trying to kill me, but it didn't take long for the mental shift to happen, and soon I was doing turns on the face. At one stage I did wear the end section of a wave on the head, and it wasn't until I looked up at it – just before it hit me – that I thought "Oh shit! Here we go…" But actually it was nowhere near what we're used to getting beaten by back home. Some of the other guys weren't so lucky, though; one wore a 50-foot peak right on the head, and another took a two-wave hold-down in the finals.

In the end, Mavericks locals Alistair Craft and Adam Replogle won the contest; Cotty and I finished 12th this time. We would have liked to have been placed in the top 10, but to be honest; I had one of the best surfs of my life that day. I loved it – it was so good to be able to surf big waves with a little less fear than usual. We aren't used to glassy smooth conditions either – when it's big back home it's windy and bumpy – so it was a real treat to experience that for a change.

Dragging myself out of the water I felt, exhausted, drained, in a daze. That night Cotty went out on a booze bender with some of the guys in the event. Hawaiian big wave surfer Alec 'Ace Cool' Cooke and Mavericks charger Tim West showed Cotty how to party in the states but all I could do was to stay awake through the prize giving. I went to the supermarket and binged on American fizzy drinks and sugary badness, then crawled straight into bed.

The energy comes in real peaks and troughs out there. I was incredibly amped, driven and excited despite being physically tired from all the travelling, the lack of sleep and food, because the end of the journey was the reward, the thought of it kept me going. But as soon as I've surfed the swell it's like a switch is flicked and I shut down almost instantaneously and completely!

Next day, and it was all over so quickly. I left on a flight just before Cotty and during the connection in Chicago he texted to tell me there was a swell due for Aileen's the day we landed. I was so tired and exhausted at this stage and I know he was too. However, plenty winters go by without us getting many really big swells so when they come along we feel like we have to take full advantage of what Mother Nature throws our way. We couldn't pass up the opportunity no matter how exhausted we were so after our flights got in we flung our gear straight in the van and drove through the night to hit Aileen's the next morning.

What a welcome home! The waves were a little smaller than the ones we rode before we left for Nelscott but we made the most of them with a couple of good paddle sessions at Aileen's and nearby Crab Island.

I still don't know how I made it home in one piece. The day long drive has strangely been wiped from my memory. I had never been so glad to crawl into my own bed and close my eyes!

The past seven days may not be everyone's idea of the perfect trip in search of surf, but for me this was the perfect end to an intense week of waves.

pound of flesh

MOST PEOPLE I KNOW think I am absolutely crazy, leaving in the middle of the night to travel to wherever big waves are forecast. It seems that the only ones who understand it are those who do it. I sometimes wonder if it's an addiction as I believe everyone has some sort of addiction be it chocolate, women, drugs or something. Maybe my addiction is to ride big waves. As cliché as it might be, I am like an addict who just needs the fix and will do anything to get it. That is so corny but it does have some relevance.

On the week beginning November 2nd, 2009 Cotty, Duncan, Paul and I were beginning to notice swell on the charts that looked like there might be a window somewhere in the week for a big wave session. We spent the week trying to second guess the forecasts. Quite often in this country we get lots of big swell but bad winds and we have kind of got to know which ones will give us a chance at surfing big waves and which ones won't. Usually the wind veers too much to the west and too strong and a lot of the big swells go unridden so we are used to getting excited and amped. Then just like when you are a kid and you are so excited about your auntie coming round on Saturday as she always brings sweets yet this time she brings you a pair of socks, we get let down. That maybe sounds childish to be bummed because the waves aren't going to be as big as forecast but to us it is what our lives revolve around. I personally can't see the pleasure in playing football more than once every now and again but I can understand how it can be the focal point of someone else's life.

So this week started off very similar to that. Cotty had gone on a magazine trip to Scotland to surf a new slab that Editor Tim Nunn had hunted out. On Friday morning we had more or less written off the next days swell forecast for Mullaghmore despite it showing in excess of seven metres. The wind just looked like it had too much west in it.

You have to understand that all of us work. So we are going about our daily routine or business and in between that we are constantly monitoring the weather charts and trying to plan meetings and work around a potential swell. My daily work routine involves working at my desk and driving around two hours every day to meetings or to check on a property or something. In between times I'm monitoring weather charts, swells, making phone calls to Cotty or organising equipment so that everything is as prepared as possible for when a big swell arrives. I am a really busy person; I don't ever feel bored nor have any time free. I pretty much allocate time slots for everything and I try to stick to it. I think it's pretty annoying for people around me as I plan out every day to the hour and I try and keep things flowing like that so I get everything done. Quite often I don't get time to spend on maintaining the ski and the equipment. It isn't uncommon for Cotty and I to be fitting something new to the ski in the dark before a session as something has worn or rusted or to be sanding down a surfboard repair. Usually we are both so busy that we don't have time to maintain all the kit and so things break rather than last and we end up replacing things instead of fixing them.

As the swell gets closer the swell and conditions get firmed up and I can begin to set meetings on days or times that fit around my surfing. It's rare that I ever have to call someone and cancel a meeting. I've usually been pretty good at planning it out so they don't even know that the day before I am sitting in their office talking about business that I was at the bottom of a 40 foot avalanche of white water running for my life.

My phone rang at 3pm on Friday afternoon as I drove back from a meeting in Belfast with my solicitor. It was Duncan. "Gigantor!!!!!" he calls out as I answered. Apparently Gigantor is some sort of comic hero

Mikee Hamilton, styling as Cotty looks on.
Photo: Aaron Pierce

that I look like or something. Duncan was also working. He had just seen the latest update on the weather charts and it looked like the wind for Saturday morning had gone more south than west possibly giving us a small window in the morning. If you have read the chapter about December 1st you will remember a similar scenario took place then giving us only a few hours to get a few bombs. I said "Look, Cotty is in Scotland at the minute, I don't think he will come so if not we can partner up and if he does then we can all rotate each other into the mix" He got straight off the phone and booked his flight over. Cotty called me minutes later saying he also had just seen the chart and he was preparing to drive the 9 hours to Mullaghmore from Thurso. We agreed that if we weren't there then we wouldn't have the chance to ride the swell if conditions worked out. We reckoned it was worth the gamble.

The next morning Duncan and I arrived in Mullaghmore at 6am to meet Cotty, Paul Okane and Mikee Hamilton. Cottys van was parked up on the headland while he tried to get a few hours sleep.

As dawn broke it was obvious that the wind was even better than forecast. It was light and although the surface looked a little bumpy from the previous days wind, it looked manageable.

We all launched our skis. Cotty and I drove ours out with Duncan on the sled. Mikee and Paul went together and their friend Dave drove the extra ski as back up.

When Cotty and I pulled up at the peak, it didn't look that big. Definitely not as big as the last few sessions we had at Aileen's and Nelscott. It didn't look that threatening. Duncan got off the sled and went and sat with Dave on the back up ski while Cotty slipped into the water and got his straps ready. "It doesn't seem as intimidating mate, maybe it's just cos we have been surfing a lot of big days lately?" He said as he lay in the water waiting for me to throw the rope out. "Yeah, you're right, just be careful anyway, no f$%kin about!" I said back and we laughed. We are always aware of how dangerous Mullaghmore is so although we felt a little more confident than normal we still planned on playing it very cautiously.

Paul and Mikee sped past us. Mikee was on the rope as Paul gunned it out towards an incoming set wave. All of us watched as Paul fired Mikee into the first wave of the day. It wasn't a gigantic wave but it threw out a cavernous barrel which most people would have avoided pulling into but Mikee leaned over and cranked a bottom turn and drove his board off the bottom and up mid face as the tube completely enclosed him. His only exit was to ride through the tube and come out the end. He pumped his board from rail to rail trying to drive it faster to make it out through the end of the tube before it collapsed in on him. We could see him in full view from where we were watching. I watched as the end section of the tube fell in front of the exit locking him into a beating for sure. Paul was following the wave looking in the white water for him unaware that he had gone down. Paul glanced over at us and we all pointed towards the impact zone to give him a heads up. Mikee surfaced and Paul got him out of there. Mikee had just recovered from a knee operation and the first wave of the session resulted in him having to sit the rest of it out. So within minutes of being out there, one of our team was downed.

I pulled Cotty up and fired him onto his first wave of the session. He got clipped by the white water and fell. He was undeterred and I took him back out for another. This time we waited for a bomb set to show up. As we waited we noticed that the reef was boiling and ledging a lot more than normal. Usually at Mullaghmore two big circular rock boils appear on the face towards the end of the ride. For some reason the swell was making the water boil up and bubble even when no waves were breaking at the time. All along the reef where the wave breaks, all in a line, these boils of water were surfacing and pouring out from below the surface. One of them was about 6 feet in diameter and surged out to about 2 feet in height. It looked like a big jelly fish. This was happening all the way along the ledge that the wave peels along. I was worried that when a huge wave comes through that the boils would get in the way and end up knocking us off.

A huge set appeared and began to explode on the headland. I swung Cotty into it from the northern side of the peak. He faded deeper to get

Paul and Duncan look on as Cotty disappears into the pit of a Mullaghmore bomb. Check out the explosion behind Cotty. *Photo*: Aaron Pierce

as close to the peak as he could. Cotty has a very graceful style when he surfs. He flows well and draws some nice lines. He disappeared into the bottom of the beast. I could see the boils bubbling up just as he went out of view. The other guys on the skis were watching from the channel as I chased the wave in case he fell. The huge end section sent plumes of water high into the sky as it exploded on the reef. I kept following it in looking for Cotty in case he fell. The other guys started pointing in towards where the big section had broken. I knew they were letting me know Cotty was down. I immediately started searching through the foam for him. I couldn't find him. There was white foam everywhere. The water was really turbulent with all the air trapped in it. He popped up about 20 feet to my right. I was still facing the ski towards shore with the next wave bearing down on me. I knew I didn't have time to get to him before the next wave hit. I hate when that happens. I knew I had to get him but I can't risk losing the ski or we are both in trouble.

I raced away from the next wave and left Cotty to take the huge white water on the head. I circled up over the shoulder of it and raced back out into an even more turbulent foam area. The water was really unstable. I knew I shouldn't have been going in there to get him. I mean the next wave was massive and again I didn't have time to get to him. At this stage he had fallen on an absolute bomb, took the second wave on the head and if I didn't get him this time, he was gonna wear a third on the head too. Normally in that situation if the wave is too close he will shout "GO GO GO!" to tell me to just leave him and come back. We do this regularly. However this was different. I kept shouting "Cotty, Cotty!" I knew there was virtually no time to get him yet he hadn't told me to go. He didn't respond to my calls. I thought something must be wrong.

The water was so frothy. It was coming up over the sides of the ski. It felt like I was in the water rather than on top of it. The next wave was a heaving 40 footer; it had just broken about 50 feet away. I couldn't get close enough to grab him and pull him on by the hand so I swung the sled at him and pointed the ski towards shore. I shouted "Cotty, grab the sled!". I had hoped that by swinging it at him he would have been able to reach out and at least grab the last loop handle on the sled. He did reach out but I wasn't close enough. The white water from the wave was roaring towards us. I had no option than to try and out run it. As I pulled the throttle the impeller started spinning but the ski didn't move. The water was so aerated and frothy that the prop wouldn't grip to get me out of there. I squeezed the throttle as Cotty disappeared into the white water just behind the ski. The ski was making a really high pitched noise as the prop span through the foam. In what was probably a split second but felt like minutes, the prop gripped and began to take off at speed. I clung on as the white water from the wave came up over the sled and brushed down my back. The ski rocked to the side as I tried to control it beneath 25 foot of white water. I had no choice than to drive at full speed and try and deal with all the boils in the surface. I gradually began to escape it and start to outrun it as it freight trained along the reef behind me. I had to run the whole way to the channel before going back to get Cotty. Cotty had surfaced and I drove in to get him, the surface wasn't as chaotic this time but it was still turbulent. I could see he looked really red in the face. Cotty always goes purple with the cold but this was different, I could see something was wrong. "Left hand, left hand" I shouted. He raised his left hand and as I came close to him I could see he was in pain "you ok?" I asked as I reached out for his hand to pull him along side the ski and onto the sled. He replied with a tone of voice that sounded like he was feeling sick "No". I moved him along the side of the ski and back to the side of the sled. As I pulled him into it his mid-section of his life vest hit into the thick foam rail. Usually we would do that and then the surfer can reach over and grab the handle. He let out a deep low moan as he pulled himself on. Thankfully there was nothing coming behind us. I drove the ski out from the impact zone slowly constantly talking to him and reassuring him that he was going to be ok. "My knee brace got ripped off and my pelvis is really sore too" he moaned. I was driving the ski sitting side on so I could see his face. He kept putting his face down on the sled. "Cotty keep looking at me, I need to see your face" "Yeah mate" he replied. I signalled to the other team that we were heading in and they started coming over to assist. "Let me compose my self first mate" Cotty said. He was considering being able to pull him self together. He tried to pull himself up onto the sled and move his joints. He had recently torn his ACL and was wearing a knee brace to support it. It had just been ripped off. His pelvis was aching from what he thought was a muscle torn. "I got folded in two when it hit me, it felt like my head nearly hit my feet!" he muttered. He was constantly saying "Mate, give me five, I'll be ok in a minute" I didn't want to be the one to say no to that but I had to "Cotty, seriously, I'm taking you in, we can sort this out on land and if you wanna come back out then that's fine but lets go in" I drove really slowly trying not to take any bumps on the ski that would move the sled and hurt him. The other teams followed in support in case we needed them. Upon arrival at the harbour he was able to stand and walk. "Go back out mate, get one of them to tow you! I'm so gutted you haven't had one yet mate!" He really wanted me to get a few yet I didn't want to leave him. He was adamant that I went back out and that he would get changed and watch from the headland. I told him that if he thinks he has to go to hospital I will come in and meet him there. His friend Lyndon was with him so he was able to get there if need be.

I drove the ski back out and watched as Paul towed Duncan for an hour or so. Duncan had a load of bombs, one after another. He also took two big avalanches on the head but was unhurt. I did water safety the whole time while Cotty watched from the van on the headland.

I gave my ski to Dave and took over driving and towed Paul. Paul is 50 years old! That is almost twice as old as some of us young guys. Let me tell you, he is just as fit as us but a whole lot wiser than most of us! Paul started off saying "Just put me on one, I just want one!" I knew this would change! I was worried that he was going to get hit too but he went on a screamer, put in a big bottom turn and pulled up mid-face and gouged it right in the pocket before riding it out to the channel! I asked "One more?" and he was like "Oh alright then!" He went on another bomb and he also rode that one out clean despite boils and ledges trying to pull his board from under his feet.

So far Paul was the only surfer to have not got hit hard that day. As we switched roles he said "Every time I drive you, it's just after you've put me on some bombs and I'm all excited, I need to settle down first!" He said as we laughed. He knew I only wanted a bomb so he waited until a good one showed up.

He drove me right into where I needed to be. I was right in the good spot, couldn't have been any better. I crossed the wake of the ski and dropped the rope. As I started to go down it, the wave didn't seem anything too out of the ordinary. Ok, if you are a non surfer then maybe this whole thing is a bit out of the ordinary but I mean it didn't appear to be the biggest bomb of the day or anything. I was about half way down it when I began to see the boils in the wave starting to pour up from the rock ledge. I was gathering speed as I was trying to work out whether they were going to get in the way of my bottom turn and take me out. Then as I looked back along the line, I could see that the wave was starting to bend around on the reef. It looked like it was closing in on me. Bt this stage I was more than two thirds of the way down it and I realised I didn't have time to put in a bottom turn or the speed to make it back up the face and chose a higher trim line to try and ride the wave out to the channel through the tube. I glanced again at the boils and they were getting closer by the second and the surface more disturbed looking. The lip of the wave began to feather way above me as I looked along the line. I then looked up over my right shoulder. This is pretty unusual to do, most of the time I am so focused on making the wave that I really only look in one direction. I must have subconsciously already admitted defeat. As I looked up over my shoulder I could see a cartoon sized wave towering above me with its lip already white capped and throwing out over me. It all happened in slow motion for me. I then looked back to the other side and it was doing the same there too. In front of me the boils were surging and the reef draining and ledging as the wave drew the water off it. I actually remember thinking "I don't know what to do!" I had two options a) jump off and try and penetrate the surface before I get hit square by a wave bigger than a house and avoid getting my ankles broken as I get smashed through my board. Or b) Straighten my board out and try and out run the lip before it lands in the hope that I clear it and get in front of it a bit like when Indiana Jones sneaks out under a slamming cave door just in the nick of time. I knew the second option was a long shot as the wave had already pitched and I was well beneath it. I stepped out of my straps to the left side of the board just before impact. The wave tubed right onto me.

BOOM! The wave exploded. Sometimes when you fall you wait for the impact. I had no waiting to do. It hit me like an articulated truck. I was concerned as I had seen the reef virtually drain just before it hit me and I thought I might end up hitting the bottom. I put my hands over my helmet to try and protect myself but the violence ripped my arms and legs out like a star fish before rag dolling me. Something glanced off the side of my helmet; I'm assuming it was my board on its way to the surface. The wave grabbed my helmet and filled it full of water like a bucket. I felt like I was being swung around underwater by King Kong holding onto my head. My chin strap was pulling tight into my jaw and throat, my eye lids and lips were getting blown open and shut. I had flashbacks of times when I had been training holding my breath. I kept thinking about the two minute mark as I knew I felt comfortable to that point and anything after that would start to concern me but that is in a controlled environment! I was in the middle of my worst wipe out to date. I had never experienced violence like this. I have said that so many times over the years as I surf bigger and bigger waves and pay higher consequences each time for doing so but this felt like I was getting charged extra!

When my two life vests popped me up to the surface I took a breath and got a mouth full of foam. I couldn't hear properly. I could only see the sky. There was so much foam at the surface I couldn't work out where I was facing so I didn't know if there was another wave coming. I got a glimpse of Paul looking for me in the white water not far away but he mustn't have seen me. I wear a bright orange helmet but I must have been under so much foam he couldn't see me even though I had my hand raised. The next one hit. I got charged down by white water. I was sent spiralling back down deep and rolled like I was in a barrel rolling down a really steep bumpy hill with no air and no idea of when it was going to stop.

This time when I surfaced I was again deep in foam and I felt cross eyed. I could just make out a ski coming in. It wasn't Paul, it was Duncan! Duncan was driving the spare ski with Dave on the back. Usually a tow team do their own rescues and having two people on the ski makes it really unstable in these conditions. I knew at this stage whatever had happened to me must have looked bad enough for Duncan to take that risk before Paul got to me. I couldn't really focus on them so I can't remember which one of them grabbed my hand to swing me onto the sled. They gunned it out before the next one hit and we made it to the channel.

That was heavy! Everyone was concerned and telling me their story of what they saw and what happened. Paul was concerned that it was his fault as he drove me onto it but I reassured him it wasn't. My head was a little sore, I could see properly but I still couldn't hear very well. I suppose the pressure must have caused that. Paul put me onto another average wave. I wasn't feeling all that good so I called it a day and sat on the sled for a while as Duncan got a couple more. Duncan fell on one doing two disco spins on his back before getting beaten and surfacing also with sore ears and blood in his mouth.

I took my helmet off and realised that the impact had cracked it! Everyone was in disbelief. We decided to call it a day after that. I was just glad it was me that got hit on the head as I was the only one of us wearing a helmet.

That entire session felt like Mrs. Mullaghmore was angry with us. She was hunting us down one by one and taking us out! She just wanted to be left alone that day. In the countless sessions I have had out there, I've never seen her in that kind of mood. She was so angry and violent.

She was definitely taking her pound of flesh for all the good rides we have had out there.

That was the first session that I really felt that everyone involved was working as a team. Up until this point all of us had spent a lot of time towing on their own. There have been lots of days were we have all been together but this day felt different, there was a real camaraderie in the air and we all had each others back. Having that bigger tight knit team in the water allows us all to be safer and ride bigger and bigger waves with extra support and confidence.

solid ground

It is Sunday night, December 13th 2009. I'm sitting in my spare room at home as I write this. I have thought about what I'm going to write for a few days now and I don't really know where to start to be honest. There is so much that has gone on and happened during the last 29 years of my life that I have really struggled to pick out the bits to write about. I have obviously focused heavily on surfing big waves in particular. One of the reasons I have for writing this book is that in Northern Ireland, surfing isn't really understood. Maybe you are a big wave surfer reading this in another part of the world where it also isn't really understood and can relate to having people ask you about it who are genuinely intrigued. This is one of the reasons I wrote this. I find it really difficult at times to explain what it is like to ride huge waves in this part of the world to someone who has no comprehension of what I am talking about. I really don't know where to start sometimes and often try and talk my way out of the conversation as quickly as possible. I figured that by writing this, all those people who want to know a bit about it can read a little bit about what it is like and what it has taken for me to ride big waves. It has been captured in photographs and videos so much and although it is really amazing to have it all documented like that I felt like actually telling the story first hand as it appears in my head would be something different.

Another reason for writing this is that I hope that one day I will have children and it might be cool for them to be able to read about their Daddy instead of just hearing me tell them stories.

I'm lucky to live in a country with such diverse seasons. We really do have four well defined seasons here in Northern Ireland and I love that.

It makes the weather more exciting and interesting. That combined with large tidal fluctuations and strong weather systems makes for some incredible waves. It does mean that the window of opportunity to ride the biggest of swells is usually small but I think that adds to the whole experience and keeps me hooked. Knowing that it is only possible to surf huge waves maybe only a handful of times in a year has got to be one of the factors that keeps me intrigued.

I hate to keep using the example of football to explain myself as I'm sure someone will think I have something against it but it is a good contrast that everyone can relate to in some way. Do you know how in football if you want to practice a particular angled kick at the goal then you can set the ball in the same place and try again and again to improve? I know there are variables such as wind etc but even that one constant of a level playing field in a sport like football is alien to surfing. There is no level playing field in surfing so it is very difficult to work on one area of surfing in particular again and again to get better at it. No two waves are the same although they may break on the same sand bank and rock ledge. The wind is always changing and the tide always moving. The Ocean demands that surfers fit into the environment around them and get to know and feel connected to it (oh, here he goes again on a corny rant I hear you say!). I'm not trying to be corny, I'm merely trying to explain how surfers have to adapt to their surroundings and be connected to what is happening around them in order to be able to surf the waves. With big waves in particular, the need for that connection is magnified. It is vital to understand the affect various wind directions, swell patterns etc have on the location at which we want to surf. That knowledge is only gained through being out there over time and is vital to allowing us to ride these waves and minimise the danger in doing so. We may get a couple of big wave sessions in a year or we may get ten if we are lucky depending on weather conditions. Can you imagine knowing that you will be playing in footballs' championship final within the next six months but not knowing exactly when until a few days out? Can you imagine not being able to practice for it other than cross training in the gym? Can you imagine not knowing if the new specially designed boots you had made will be up to it on the day? It would be pretty unnerving going into that big game with all those doubts and not much practice wouldn't it? Well that is kind of how this is for me. Yes I can go surfing everyday of the year, and I always try to. And, yes I can cross train etc too but this doesn't completely prepare me for the gut wrenching fear and doubts in myself that I feel when I paddle out in 30 to 40 foot surf or take the jet ski out for the first time in three or four months. It doesn't prepare me for the first time I take out my new 10'8" gun and I'm half way down the face of a 40 foot Mullaghmore sledge hammer hoping that it will allow me to turn at the bottom of the wave to avoid getting smashed by the lip as the surf hasn't been big enough to have used it before.

People regularly say to me "Oh, the waves are too small for you today surely?" when they see me heading out at Castlerock or East Strand for a surf in two foot onshore mushy waves. What they don't realise is that it is through being comfortable in smaller surf, regardless of the conditions that has allowed me to pursue my dream of riding huge waves. Being in the sea so much that it feels more like home than my own sofa does, is what has allowed me to live my dreams ever since I was 13 watching the Monster Mavericks video with my brother.

I do believe that surfing has been the solid ground in my life, besides my family around me that is. Surfing has always been there for me regardless of failed friendships, relationships, losing my father and all the other things that we all have to face in life. It has always been there for me. I always try to protect my ability to surf. As long as I have the physical ability to at least catch small waves for as long as I live, I think I will remain sane. It is and has been a release for me from ordinary life and I'm sure other people have some sort of release too. Surfing is a good clean sport, which has given me something to focus on and has taken me so many places and allowed me to push my own personal boundaries and discover things about myself I may never have known otherwise. It may be the reason that I was so able to cope with losing my father and all that came with it.

One thing which really sticks out in my mind is my memory of me surfing as a child at Castlerock. Castlerock breaks further and further out to sea, the bigger the surf gets. To get out the back, it can take battling through white water waves for up to 30 minutes. Sometimes it feels like I will never get out the back because so many waves are pushing me back and holding me on the inside near the shore. I suppose that is like life and sometimes when I'm working or something is frustrating me then that memory pops into my head. I know if I keep persevering I will eventually break through the white water and get out the back and catch a really good wave. I know that fighting through the white water is worth it once I get out there and get a big one. It is the same in life. So many things get us down and hold us back. If you really want something you do have to fight for it sometimes. So many obstacles can get in the way and at anytime you can give in and walk away but you won't get what you want then. Perseverance is so important if you want to get something that means a lot to you. Being strong enough to keep fighting for it and not to walk away at the first sign of defeat can be difficult however to give up can be painful. I heard a quote on television one time by an American Football player. He said "There are two types of pain, pain of discipline and pain of regret" That has popped into my head a few times over the years.

When we lost the ski that was the optimum time for us to put our hands up, admit defeat and walk away but it actually made us stronger and we fought harder than ever. I think with big wave surfing in particular and probably life too, although I'm not that old to be wise enough to comment confidently on that, I think I have learned to roll with the punches so to speak. It is virtually impossible to go out into the ocean in huge waves, sneak into a few paddling or towing, have the ride of your life and come back in and put the fire on. It doesn't happen like that, wipe outs occur, mis-timings result in beatings, equipment fails, we fail. As nice as it would be to go out there and ride a huge wave without all the complications and mishaps; they are all part of it. They are the price we have to pay to ride these waves. That is also true of life in that success comes with a price be it financially, physically, emotionally or our health. Cotty jokes about us writing a book called 'The Book of Big Wave Surfing F%^k Ups' but honestly we could do it. We've lost a ski, flooded the van twice, ran over ropes, missed flights, both wheels have come off the trailer while driving, got myself smashed on the rocks, Cotty tore his ACL, pulled muscles, I cracked my helmet, I've been run over by the ski, our winch has broken, the list goes on…It is all part of it and is what keeps us so intrigued. I can only speak for myself although I regularly write 'we' throughout this book because I don't see myself without Cotty being involved in some way.

Cotty is the most dedicated surfer I know. I mean he jumps on flights to come over here to surf big waves with me all the time. He leaves his work, family and girlfriend regularly so we can play in the sea like kids! I suppose to Cotty's girlfriend she must think there's another woman that he's not telling her about as he disappears at the drop of a hat or in the middle of the night. She is probably wondering if I actually exist and if he is just coming over to see his bit on the side. Honestly, Cotty is an amazing person. He is so strong and loyal. We have never had a raised word between us or fought about anything. We speak on the phone on average about twice a day. That might be hard to believe but seriously we do. If there is a swell on the charts we would speak up to 10 or 12 times in a day! Recently my brother came to watch us surf one day and later commented on us as a team. It was 6am and we were standing in the rain and dark at Doolin harbour. I was buzzing around getting everything ready but Cotty was feeling really sick, he had his knee all braced up wasn't feeling up for it at all. He was adamant that we went out anyway. My brother made him a hot cup of soup to warm him up and Cotty said "I'm feeling so shit, I don't want to go out but Al is frothing as usual so we are going" It wasn't said in a way that he was being dragged out there by me, it was said in a way that made Andrew realise that Cotty would do anything for me. He was feeling sick and didn't feel up to it but he didn't want me to miss out on a good session. Cotty spent 6 hours in the water that day; he got towed into a couple of waves but sat on the ski more or less the whole time to keep an eye on me while I paddled two different sessions. He even towed Paul into a bunch of waves in between times. I have so many good things to say about Cotty. I'm glad I met someone who shared a similar passion to me. There are times when I don't want to go on a big one and I can see his face looking at me with a look of "GOOOOO!" in his eyes. Having someone who has faith and believes in me and vice versa is an amazing feeling and pushes me and I'm sure him to higher levels. It can be so easy to be paddling for a monster or be towed into a monster and seeing the sheer size and volume of water and thinking "NO f$%kin way!" and pulling back even though I have been in that situation a million times before and not had a second thought. Sometimes that wee bit of fear just takes over and creates doubt but having a solid partner to surf with has pushed both of us to commit and overcome situations and deal with fear together.

It is obvious that as surfing progresses with each generation of surfers, the extremes and boundaries of the sport are pushed out by everyone involved to varying degrees. The progression of paddling into big waves may have somewhat been slowed due to the advent of tow surfing but

recently the limit is rising of what is considered humanly catchable by paddling without the assistance of a jet ski. I personally love paddling big waves more so than towing them. Yes, I do love all the camaraderie and the team work involved with towing but paddling is where my true passion lies. I just love being out there with a huge board. It makes me feel challenged and is so rewarding to catch a huge wave and dealing with all the emotions that I go through in order to ride one on my own. I began by surfing largely on my own in big waves and following that right through to tow surfing. I do believe that this country in particular is particularly suited to tow surfing due to the windy and bumpy conditions we get which can make paddling difficult at some spots. However, I do hope to continue pushing my paddle in surfing limits to new heights too. I hope that my involvement in the sport has been and continues to be a part of its progression.

Above: **This is me paddling into a wave at Aileens October 2009.**
Photo: Gary McCall

Left: **Duncan comes to give me 5!**
Photo: Aaron Pierce

acknowledgements

Special Thanks to all the photographers and videographers who have worked with us, giving up their time and spending their own cash to come and capture us on film…

Anthony Butler, Aaron Pierce, Kelly Allen, Tony Plant, Tony Canadas, Al MacKinnon, Mike Newman, Ester Spears, Ben Granata, Tim Ditty, Gary McCall, Conn Osborne, Johnny Vance, Justin Avery, Joe Kennedy, Jamie Russell, Remy Whiting, Roger Sharp, Mickey Smith, Rob Keith

Mum – Thanks for supporting me and believing in me and trusting that I will always play it safe.

Dad – Thank you Dad, thanks for all the love and opportunities that you gave us. My world is not the same without you. I would give anything to have you here today. Thanks for always believing in me and never doubting me. You are my hero and my idol.

Andrew – Thanks for always believing in me.

Cotty – Cotty, you are the man! Without you things would be very different. Thank you for giving me your time, your friendship, your trust, your dedication, your camaraderie. Without you I would be lost. We have been through so much together and sometimes I think we forget how much we have dealt with as we are always so immersed in it. Writing this book has given me the chance to recount some of the best times in my life and highlighted the fact that having you as a friend has been one of the best things that ever happened to me.

Leah - Thank you for supporting me and being there for me in all that I do. You put a lot of time into reading this as I was writing it and your input was vital. Thank you. You are a breath of fresh air.

Alan Simpson - thank you for always giving me air time and for supporting me throughout the years. You are an inspiration to many!

Andrew Wilson - for putting up with me phoning you every Saturday morning at 630am trying to convince you that you should come and surf with me!

Anthony Butler - for finding us interesting enough to eat crackers for two years so that you could film us. Thank you!

Anton Roberts - for being the other big guy at all the events and lending me your board at the nationals!

Barry 'Baz' Johnston - for supporting me at all times and always being prepared to do anything for me! Thank you.

Ben Granata - for your continued friendship!

Gareth Beckett – Thanks for the hardcore driving and for seeing the potential. It was always good to have you there!

Carl - for your time, support, and balls!I don't think either of us will forget that first Mullaghmore tow wave! Thanks for putting yourself out there and for going through all the mishaps!

Chris Little - a true friend. One of those people who I don't see or hear from very often but I just know you would do anything for me! Thanks mate.

Coleraine Chronicle and Coleraine Times - Milne Rowntree, Peter Winter, Damian Mullan, Richard Baker, Davey Rankin, Kyle White thanks for finding me interesting enough to warrant so much coverage in your papers! You truly have supported me since way back when Andrew and I were young kids. Thank you very much.

Dave Reed - for your vision and belief in British Surfing. You are a true Living Legend and the progression of surfing is hugely down to you putting your self out there even when the surf industry wouldn't support you with funding for your events. You are extremely passionate about surfing and the well being of all the surfers. Thank you for accepting me into the scene when I started out in your events and for all the good you have given to this sport. I salute you!

Duncan Scott - for your surfing, vision, belief and knowledge. There is no doubt, you are solid in the water. I never doubt your ability. You always appear so comfortable whatever the conditions! It is reassuring to be in the water with you.

Emmet for so many things - I actually don't know where to begin. For supporting me when Dad died, for sharing my vision. Going on that trip to Mavericks changed everything. It was the most significant point in surfing for me and to have you share in that dream was amazing. You are one of my oldest friends and I can't wait for our next paddle sesh at you know where!

Eric Akiskalian - for your unrivalled support. You have helped both Cotty and I continually across the years, always fought our corner and stood up for us. I thank you greatly; you are a wonderful man with a big heart.

Francie McGreevy - for believing in me, for seeing the potential in me and being more committed to my Mum, Andrew and I than anyone else. Dad would have been so happy that you were there for us all, I can't thank you enough. You are an exceptionally kind man and I know you would do absolutely anything for us all. Thank you dearly.

Robert Hamilton - Thank you for all you do for us. I am so lucky to have you to bounce things off and ask for advice. You have in many ways been there for me and have shone light into the darkness and shown me a way forward. Thank you.

Peter Nicholle - for supporting me from way back! You are a wonderful individual, loved by many. I know you are there at anytime and would do anything for me without a thought! Thank you Pete!

Howard Robinson - for your support, your interest and your belief.

Jamie Russell – Thanks for your friendship, your support and interest in me!

Joe Kennedy - for your vision and your time!

Kay Collins - You have been unbelievable. While Francie had the site covered you had the office covered. We couldn't have done it without you. We owe you so much and I am so glad you were about when it happened. You are easy to get on with and you treated us with a personal approach. Thank you for your support.

Kieran Clancey - for noticing that Ireland had big waves and supporting the few of us that ride them.

Killian O'Kelly - thanks for putting us up and always making sure we are sorted even when we arrive in the middle of the night-sorry Tony!

Malachy Murray - for your support and personal approach. You believed in me and talking to you on the site made the darkness a little brighter!

Mark Miller - for support from day one.

Mark Patterson - you are one of the most genuine people I know. Thanks for your support and interest in me.

Martin Pierce - for including me

Mikee Hamilton – Thanks for your energy and enthusiasm!

Mike and Sarah Gerhardt - thank you for showing me the ropes, giving me your knowledge, selling me a board. Thank you for helping me realise my dream. I owe so much to your support!

Paul Okane - for being onboard even on days when you don't have a partner, always being involved and making sure we all are safe. I love surfing with you.

Simon McKivor - Thanks mate. You have been there through thick and thin over the last few years. You understand me like no one else! You are great with people and a real friend.

Richard Fitzgerald – Thanks for inspiring me and for sharing in some of the sessions and madness.

Ronan Harkin - for providing the weapons!

Xelements Magazine
Pitpilot Magazine
Carve magazine
Wavelength magazine
Circle One
Jeff Townlsey
Jeff Sacree
Doug Black
Alan Gilchrist
Pete and Dave at West
Haley Fiske
Chris Curry
Neil Hamilton
Ali out n about
Adele Shaw
Andy Hill
Briohny Fitzgerald
Mark Wilson
Mark McKeeman
Rodhri Jones
Carlos Burle
Garth Stalford
A1 surf
Beach bum
Jason Ribbink
Gigs Celliers
Bill Sharp
The Morgans
Angela Rivers at Drift Magazine
Chris Nelson and Demi Taylor at
footprint publications
Lindsays outdoor wear Coleraine
Pete Jump
Steve Wright
Johnny Bingham
Martin Kelly
Justin Avery
Brent Hudson
Steven Scullion
Rosin at Outsider Magazine
BBC

UTV
Ollie Boyd
Sharon Cross
Ricky McCarther
Steve, and the Ritchies
Liam and Joey Lynch
Ricky Woodside
Mike Smith
Barry Mottershead
Gary McCall
Ralph and Shay Freeman
Jules
Neil Perrow
Gethin Jones
Chris Bertish
Wayne Clegget
John Owen
Dan Wilson
Ernie Capbert
Ryan Glass
Kevin Ridsdale
Nick Blair
Nick and Andy Soper
Finn Mullen
Fergus Stevenson
Rodney Kilborne
Adam Wagner
Oscar Gomez
Seiss
Graham Campbell
Alan Barber
Al Nicol
Alex Wade
Richard Hallman
Steven Banks
Ben Nash at iextv
Ben Farwagi
Dan Joel
Ben Skinner
Ben Marcus
Thomas at Blue Magazine

Todd-Dolan Smith
Donna Trainor
Sarah Dobson
Clifford Gow
Derek Hynd
Karen Patterson
Graham at Freeride Ireland
Howling Dog Productions
Roo McCrudden
Lorcan McFadden
Greg Martin
Remy Whiting
Gemma Harris
Mark Hamill
Davey Moore
Phil Ireland
Nathan Hill
Jessica Lepoidevin
John Hibbard
David Somerville
Joe Moran

Daz Wright
Larry Jansky
Alan Stokes
Russell Winter
Spencer Hargreaves
Shawn Alladio
Karen Walton
Nolan McSkimming
Stuart Norton
Owen Conlon
Scott Winer
Tim Spicer
Craig Watson
Mark Visser
Ross Olphart
Scott and Johnny Laverty
Ryan McCafferty
Ronan McSharry
Lloyd Russell
Matt Dale
Sheila Kyle

Websites

www.almennie.com
www.westsurfing.com
www.rosysurfboards.com
www.extremenutrition.co.uk
www.geckoheadgear.com
www.mrbproductions.co.uk
www.drivendoc.com
www.towsurfer.com
www.surfersvillage.com
www.A1surf.com

DVDs / Movies

Driven – Mr B Productions
Performing Monkeys – Mr. B Productions
Waveriders – Besom Productions

glossary of terms

Tube/Barrel – The space created between the falling lip of the wave and the face of the wave often forms as a tube or barrel type cylinder of water.

Bomb – used to describe a big wave in that it is similar to a bomb in many ways.

Beach break – waves which break on a sandy bottom

Reef – waves which break on a rocky bottom maybe on boulders or a rock ledge

Boil – term used to describe water movement at the surface which is created by holes, caves or boulders sitting up on the reef under water.

Tow surfing – term used to describe when two big wave surfers team up to utilise a pwc/jet ski to catch waves that are too big and fast moving to catch by conventional paddle power alone.
Tow straps - straps screwed into the deck of a tow board to keep the surfers feet from moving on the board.

Tow board – specially designed surf board to suit big wave surfing, using a jet ski.

Gun – a big wave board used to paddle into big waves.

Hollow – used to describe waves with tubes

Lip – the crest of the wave

Lagoon – area of still water behind a reef, rocks or islands.

Point break – A headland of rock or sand protruding out into the ocean which causes the waves to break along it gradually rather than cause them to break all at once.

Closing out – a wave that breaks all at once is referred to as closing out and doesn't allow the surfer to ride the open face.

Bottom turn – a turn a surfer does at the bottom of the wave to propel him either back up the face of the wave or along the line of the wave.

Peel – A peeling wave is one that doesn't close out.

Rail – The rail of the surfboard is its edges.

Kicking out – surfers kick out of a wave at the end of a ride, it basically means the surfer finishes their ride and pulls off the shoulder of the wave.

Shoulder – The shoulder of a wave is next to the curl or tube, it is a less critical or steep section of the wave.

Channel – Deep water beside a shallow bank of sand or reef that is too deep for the waves to break. The channel is often used as a safety zone in big surf or for access to the main peak of the waves without having to go directly through the centre zone of the surf.

Curl – A curl is formed when a wave breaks, the shape it forms looks like a curl when viewed from the side.

Pocket – The Pocket relates to the space beneath the falling lip of the wave.

Trim line – The path a surfer takes across the wave.

Draining – The reef might drain which means the water gets drawn off it to varying degrees by the force of the wave as it stands up before breaking.
At some spots the wave can completely suck the reef dry and at others the wave might not even have the draining effect.

Pitch – The lip of the wave throws out or pitches into the air as it breaks.